I Am Asking God
to Meet You at the
Point of All your needs
and Manifest His Miracle-
working Power for your
Every Need!,

Morris Cerullo

i

The Miracle Book

Now, Lord – Stretch out your hand to heal and perform miraculous signs and wonders through the name of your holy servant Jesus.

(Acts 4:29-30, NIV)

Dear Friends,

God would not have put so many promises in His written Word that require divine intervention if He did not plan to manifest Himself to us through **miracles**.

This book is the result of my personal experiences with Almighty God and His Son, our Lord and Savior Jesus Christ. **You** can experience a breakthrough to where your life becomes a rhythm of miracles, rather than miracles being the exception.

May God's miracle – working power flow through every aspect of your life – your home, your job, your family, your friends, your relationships, your finances, your spiritual life, your physical body – as you experience a spiritual breakthrough that will penetrate to new dimensions.

You will enter into a rhythm of Miracle Power Living. It will be as natural for you to experience miracles every day as it is to eat, breathe, and sleep.

This is God's will for all His people, in Jesus' Name.

Beloved, I wish above all things that thou mayest prosper and be in health, even as thy soul prospereth. (III John 1:2)

God's servant,

The Miracle Book

The Miracle Book

How you can live in a rhythm of miracles using 5 simple steps

Published by

Morris Cerullo World Evangelism, Inc.

San Diego, California

First Printing • May 1984
Second Printing • 1987
Third Printing • 1992
Fourth Printing • 1995
Fifth Printing • 1997
Sixth Printing • 2000
Seventh Printing • 2006
Copyright © 1984
Morris Cerullo World Evangelism
Printed in U.S.A.

Table Of Contents

Dr. Morris Cerullo, President
MORRIS CERULLO WORLD EVANGELISM

I Believe In A God Of Miracles

My purpose in writing this book is two-fold: 1) to share with you how you can reach out and receive a miracle from God at the point of your need: and 2) to show you how it is possible for you to live in a miracle realm as naturally as you breathe, where miracles become a normal part of your day-to-day existence.

I realize it is hard for most people to relate to miracles. Miracles seem out of reach, unattainable. It is not so much a matter of believing God is able to perform a miracle as much as it is that they feel they do not have enough faith to reach God and believe for a miracle in their own life.

You may feel a miracle is out of your reach. You may not know how to approach God regarding the needs in your life. You may not even have a clear understanding of what a miracle really is.

From my own personal experience I can tell you that I did not know anything about supernatural manifestations and the miracles of God except what I had read in the Old Testament, and that in a historical context only. But then, God came to me at the point of my deepest need at the age of eight. I was ready to jump to my death from the window ledge of an orphanage. I was lonely, scared. I had given up all hope. God came to me at that point of deep desperation and miraculously intervened. His Presence filled the room behind me, and He spoke peace and comfort to me. His comforting Presence assured me that He loved me, and He gave me a reason to live. He stopped me from committing suicide.

Later in my life, at the age of 14 1/2, God once again intervened by supernaturally leading me out of the orphanage to a place in front of the Montauk Theatre, where I met the Christian woman who had been instrumental in leading me into an experience of accepting Jesus Christ into my heart. Right away, I was given a place to live in the home of her brother and his wife.

At that point in my life, if anyone had told me that God was going to use me to stand before some of the largest crowds in the history of Christianity, to speak as a prophet and apostle to the nations, and to train hundreds of thousands of Nationals in over 130 countries around the world to reach their nations for God, I would have told them they were crazy.

I had no intention of becoming a minister of the Gospel. My driving ambition was to one day become governor of my state of New Jersey.

But one night in an old Presbyterian church, as I knelt at the altar, God supernaturally revealed Himself to me and changed the course of my life.

As I was kneeling down, I could feel the pressure of a hand on my forehead. Suddenly, I found myself flat on my back.

I was conscious and could hear the noise of the people around me, but I felt paralyzed. I tried to get up but I couldn't. I tried to move my hands and my legs but I was unable to move.

As I lay there on the floor in this condition, my spirit was taken out of my body. The next thing I knew, I was in the heavens.

In the heavens, I saw a multitude of people that no man could number, stretched out as far as my eyes could see to the right and left of the horizon, of every nationality: red, yellow, black, and white. These people appeared to be seated in a semi-circle configuration, even though they had no chairs.

As I looked upon this great multitude, my spirit entered a body on the front row, which I recognized as my own physical body. It is humanly impossible to describe with my tongue. There are no words, in any of languages of the world, to describe what I saw next. Suddenly, in front of this tremendous multitude of people, the glory of God appeared. The Form that I saw was about the height of a man six feet tall, maybe a little taller, and twice as broad as a human body but with no distinguishing features, such as eyes, nose, or mouth. This Form shone with the flaming brightness of a million moons, a million suns, and billions of stars in one.

As my eyes were beholding this great manifestation of God's glory, a ray about three or four times the diameter of a man's arm shot out from this glorious Form and struck my being. The ray of light was like a magnet, pulling me forward, drawing me closer and closer toward this manifested Presence of God.

Now, you must remember, I knew absolutely nothing about the supernatural power of God. I was only fifteen at the time. I was an orphan, a stranger now in a world where I knew only one or two people.

During this entire experience I was in a state of absolute consciousness. Thoughts were rushing through me like wind. I was sensing tremendous emotions: fear, anxiety, and perplexity, coupled with tremendous joy and exhilaration.

As I was savoring this moment, basking in the tremendous love and glory that emanated from this glorious Being, the glory of God moved one step away from me. My heart sank! I couldn't understand it. I was confused. In my heart I was thinking, Lord, You drew me up here. I was standing by Your side and now You have walked one step away from me.

Then something constrained me to look down where the Presence of God had moved away from me, and I saw in the heavens, cut out of the sky, a hole in the form of two footprints.

I looked through that hole, and what I saw changed my life. It was as if God had taken the lid off of hell and allowed me to see from heaven down into the portals of the underworld. I saw the flames of fire that will never be quenched. I heard the cries of the damned and the lost. I felt the torment of the backslider; his cry was the worst of all.

I knew when I saw those footprints in the sky that I had a choice. God was saying to me, "Morris, will you give Me your life?" As I heard those cries, and saw the eternal damnation of souls in an eternity without God, I yielded and surrendered everything to God and put my feet in those footprints.

A warmth came around my shoulders. I turned, and the glory of God had taken the ray that had drawn me to Him and had placed that ray around my shoulders. My whole body became like a luminous paint. It lit up from the top of my head to the soles of my feet.

And then, for the first time, God spoke. A voice came out of the glory of God and spoke words to me I had never heard before, but which I later discovered were taken from the Old Testament book of Isaiah 60:1: *Arise and shine for My light is come upon thee and the glory of the Lord shall surround thee, for the multitude of the sea of the Gentiles shall be converted unto thee.*

From this glorious, manifested Presence of God, rays shot out over the heads of the people and they literally lit up the heavens and those people. God spoke to me again: *Son, when you see My glory in the midst of My people, and as you stand before them, then know that I am there to show Myself strong in behalf of them that love Me.*

This experience as a young boy was only the beginning. Throughout my current 60 years of ministry to the nations of the world, I have watched God show Himself strong on behalf of those who love Him, just as He said He would during that tremendous encounter with Him.

I have watched God as He has restored sight to the blind, opened deaf ears, healed the lame, and performed miracle after miracle in response to the cries of people around the world.

Yes, without a doubt, with every fiber of my being I can say to you today that I believe in a God of miracles. He has revealed Himself to me. I have seen His glory. He has always been and will always be a God of miracles.

As I look back over the experiences where God has revealed Himself through miracles in my life and in the lives of thousands of others, I can now understand one of the reasons why He took a small boy from the state of New Jersey and sent him to the four corners of the Earth.

In every miracle that I have experienced, and in every miracle God has allowed me to witness, He has been planting a seed in my life. Over these 60 years of witnessing miracle after miracle, He has been preparing me for a day when I would be able to share with people everywhere how they can receive a miracle in their lives, and not only receive miracles but live a life filled with one miracle after another.

That day is here. God is now using these experiences to bring forth the truths presented in this book.

For many years now the Spirit of God has been bringing more clearly into focus within my spirit new insights concerning miracles, as well as five simple steps based on the Word of God which will unlock some of the mysteries and questions you may have concerning miracles, such as:

Are miracles for today?

Is the day of miracles past?

Does God perform miracles to prove himself?

Will God perform a miracle in my life?

How can I have the faith to believe God for a miracle?

Can I really expect God to reach out to me right where I am - reguardless of the mess I've made out of my life - and meet me at the point of my need and work a miracle on my behalf?

As you read , I want you to focus your mind on two very important point:

1.God is and always will be a miracle-working; and
2. Yes, God can and will perform the miracle you need.

In this book, I am sharing not only from the wealth of experiences God has given me as a servant of God, but I will be sharing with you personal experiences about how God came to me when I had no one else to turn to, when I didn't know what to do. God met me at the point of my deepest need, and He will meet you there, too.

Regardless of who you are, what you may have done, where you may have been, or how great your need, the one thing that qualifies you for a miracle is that you have a need.

As you apply the five steps to miracles I will be sharing with you, you will be able to reach out and receive the miracle you need and enter into a new realm of living.

Why? Because God always has been and always will be a God of miracles.

Chapter One

You Were Made For Miracles

God wants you to live in a new rhythm, a new way of life where miracles are a natural occurrence. Whether it is a miracle providing food for you and your family – whether it is a miracle directing you where to go – whether it is showing you what or how to do something – or whether it is a miracle of healing, your life can be filled with miracles.

As unbelievable as it may seem to you right now, it is possible!

Miracles are real, and you can have them in your life. I can make that statement because God has taken me step by step from my early childhood and has taught me how to live a life filled with one miracle after another.

In learning to trust God for miracles, it has not been easy. I have faced some very difficult situations, as you will see from the personal experiences I will be sharing with you later in this book. God has always been faithful. Not one time has He ever failed me, and I know that He never will!

I realize that it is difficult for most people to relate to miracles. The average person may have heard or read somewhere in a book or magazine about an occasional miracle happening. They may have heard a personal testimony of a miracle healing on a Christian television program, or they may have been taught as a young child in Sunday School how God performed miracles for the nation of Israel and how Jesus performed miracles while He was on Earth. But the average person has never seen or experienced a miracle in their own life.

There are many reasons why most people have never experienced a miracle, but underneath these reasons we see the root cause.

Man is limited by his own personal environment.

The level on which most humanity lives limits them from entering into a rhythm of miracles because their expectancy level is not at the point where they are looking for a daily manifestation of God's miracle power to flow through their lives.

Man is a product of his environment. He is limited by what he hears, speaks, observes, and by what he is taught.

Somehow man has regressed from the New Testament days when miracles were a normal occurrence. Everywhere Jesus' disciples went miracles followed. They were ***expected***. Jesus had told them that miracles would be a normal part of their lives, that signs and wonders would follow all those who believe (Mark 16:17-18).

As the years passed, man began to teach that miracles ceased with the apostles, that miracles were no longer necessary, and that people should not seek after miracles. And in more recent years, secular humanism has permeated our society in an attempt to explain away the miracle of creation and other miracles as recorded in the Bible, as well as miracles that are happening today.

This teaching and influence over the years has infiltrated our society and many of our churches. As a result, man's expectancy level remains at a point that hinders him from experiencing miracles on a consistent basis.

In foreign countries where this teaching and humanistic philosophy has not been propagated throughout the years, the expectancy level is much higher. When the people hear that God wants to perform a miracle of salvation or healing, they respond in a simple, childlike faith, and miracles happen in great numbers on a consistent basis.

You are a product of your own personal environment. What you have observed and what you have been taught affects your level of expectancy and can hinder you from receiving the miracle you need.

God lifted me out of a traditional environment, where miracles were relegated to historical events, and has raised my level of expectancy to where I look for God to perform miracles in my life on a daily, consistent basis. And I believe He will do the same for you as we look at some of the questions many people have concerning miracles.

What Is A Miracle?

Because man is a product of his environment, most people do not have a clear understanding of what a miracle is.

Miracles seem to be far out of reach and it is hard for people to grasp something so supernatural and so unfamiliar to them.

Many years ago, I asked God to give me a clear definition of miracles that I could share with people to help them break through their personal environment and see clearly what miracles are. He gave me this very simple definition:

A miracle is something which cannot happen by human means.

Most people's concept of a miracle is the way a car runs or the way an airplane or spaceship flies. Our homes are full of what we often refer to as twentieth century miracles: electricity, dishwashers, disposals, microwave ovens, and computers.

These are not miracles, even though they have been labeled as such.

Polio and diphtheria vaccines, insulin, laser beam surgery, test-tube babies, and artificial limbs are man's medical discoveries. They are not miracles. Why?

Because each one of these natural discoveries can be explained. There is a logical explanation that can be understood by man's intellect. Man has made a breakthrough in the natural world. He has passed through whatever was holding back the knowledge to create, design, and produce what seemed to be impossible. Once the breakthrough came – wham! Man had electricity, cars, airplanes, penicillin, etc.

All of these breakthroughs came as a result of man's ability and his own inner natural resources. However, a miracle is something that goes beyond man, beyond ourselves. Its root lies in the fact that it is something which cannot happen by human means.

Miracles are not the work of a man. Regardless of man's increasing mental capabilities or technological breakthroughs, man cannot produce a miracle.

Others say it is an outstanding healing that someone receives. Actually, the healing is a product of God's miracle power. It is the end result.

A miracle is a supernatural manifestation of God that comes into our daily lives to deal with events and circumstances that cannot be met by just the normal means.

Most people have at one time or another faced a problem relating to money, so, as an example, let's use a hypothetical circumstance regarding finances.

Let's suppose the rent or payment on your house is due. You have been out of work with little or no income and do not have enough money to put food on the table, much less pay the rent. There is no one you can turn to for a loan. There appears to be no solution, no way out. What do you do?

If you are living in a daily expectancy of miracles, God can and will supernaturally provide. He will send an angel, if necessary, with the money, or He may use someone else as an instrument to give you the miracle you need.

In the New Testament, the disciples faced a financial crisis. They didn't have the money to pay their taxes. They came to Jesus and He miraculously met that need by preparing a fish with the needed money in its mouth (Matthew 17:24-27). When you have a need, don't limit God! Allow Him to provide for your needs in any manner He chooses. Expect Him to work miracles daily as the need arises.

Miracles are the natural characteristic of God. People look at miracles as the exception, but God is trying to teach us that miracles should be the normal experience of our lives because God's character is to perform miracles. He doesn't do anything contrary to His nature, and therefore, miracles are not unnatural; they are a natural flow of God's love for us.

Remember, a miracle is something that cannot happen by human means. When you receive a miracle from God, you cannot explain it. You do not question. You must simply accept it. You do not know how it happened, but God did it, and that settles it. The key is coming into an experience in your life where you expect God to intervene in your daily needs.

Are Miracles For Today?

It is one thing to believe that God performed miracles four thousand years ago, or even two thousand years ago, but it is quite another to believe that God still performs miracles today. Because they do not understand God's purpose for performing miracles, some people do not believe that miracles are for today.

One day, during a meeting I was conducting, a minister (who was a graduate of one of the biggest theological seminaries in America) came to me. He said, "Mr. Cerullo, why don't you stop fooling the people?"

I was rather startled and puzzled by this question, and I replied, "What do you mean, sir?" He said, "You know that the day of miracles is past. There's no such thing as a day of miracles."

I looked at him and said, "Sir, that's true." He was a little stunned by my answer, and he replied, "What? I thought you were praying for the sick." I said, "I am. I do."

Not knowing what to expect next, he said, "Well, how can you do that if you don't believe in a day of miracles?" I said, "You and I have nothing to argue about because I believe the same as you do. I don't believe in a day of miracles." And I don't.

There is no "day of miracles." There is only a God of miracle-working power.

When Jesus Christ was revealed to me, it was not difficult for me to believe that God is Who He claims to be. I was taught about the Jewish people who served a God Who appeared in pillars of clouds by day and pillars of fire by night. He opened the Red Sea, and fed them from heaven for 40 years in a wilderness. He rolled back the River Jordan. He walked into the lions' den and closed the lions' mouths.

I believe in a God of miracles Who is the same every day!

We must not worship days. We cannot look back and say that four thousand or two thousand years ago was a day of miracles.

God is a supernatural God, and He is the same yesterday, today, and forever (Hebrews 13:8). Men change. Church structure changes. Theology changes. God does not change.

From man's existence in the Garden of Eden until today, God's methodology of revealing Himself and dealing with His people has not changed. He is not a God of dispensation or time. He has no beginning and no ending.

To give you an example of how man's theology is subject to change, let's consider what God is doing at a leading theological seminary to break through man's theory that the day of miracles is past.

Years ago, at the School of World Missions at Fuller Theological Seminary, C. Peter Wagner, Professor of Church Growth, introduced a new course for study titled "Signs, Wonders, and Church Growth," taught by the late Professor John Wimber.

Students who enrolled in this new course not only studied the biblical and historical basis for "Signs and Wonders," but also in the classroom they allowed the Gifts of the Spirit to function and began laying hands on the sick. The result? Miracles happened! The course became one of the most popular subjects the seminary ever offered, with wall-to-wall students in the largest room on campus.

The members of the faculty were from many different backgrounds: United Presbyterian, Mennonite, Brethren, United Methodist, Reformed Presbyterian, Congregational Bible Church.

One of the reasons they decided to offer this course is that their studies in church growth on the mission field indicated that the major growth came as a result of the manifestation of the miracle-working power of God, a result of miracles that are happening *today*.

Here are a few excerpts taken from the book, based on the reactions of the faculty and students who attended the course:

> David and Eva Brougham, missionaries in Southeast Asia, are Presbyterian, and their theological training is strongly grounded in conservative, dispensational evangelism. They did not believe that miracles could occur today. They did not believe that healing and deliverance were meant for the present. To them, these things happened in Jesus' lifetime, but not now.
>
> Yet, their experiences on the mission field contradicted the theory they had learned in the seminary classrooms. They saw people healed.
>
> They saw people delivered from demon oppression. They saw people experience a special, second blessing from the Holy Spirit. The Broughams witnessed God working in the world *today*.
>
> David and Eva decided they needed to relearn their theology, to correlate their theology with their experiences.

They had heard about Fuller's course on "Signs, Wonders, and Church Growth" and decided to become involved.

In an interview here is what David Brougham said when asked if it had been necessary to unlearn any prejudices or presuppositions that he held:

> "What I did not learn until I got into hard difficult situations on the field was that God is alive and working today. So my dispensational views had to undergo some changes. I saw things that happened in the Bible happening today. I had to go back and rethink my theology, especially concerning the Person and work of the Holy Spirit.
>
> "I've come to realize that Jesus' works and words are still applicable today as they were yesterday."

Charles Kraft, Professor of Intercultural Communications and African studies at Fuller, attended the course. Here are some excerpts from his evaluation of the course:

> "We are taught that miracles and healing are not part of our experience. Such things ended in the first century, and we'll never experience them. From this background we go to conservative colleges, then to the mission field. There we find that, very often, God is doing these things...
>
> "I don't believe that miracles have ever been absent from our culture. I think our eyes have been clouded over so that we haven't seen things. When people open themselves up to more of the miraculous, I feel that God gives it to them."[1]

Many others attending the "Signs, Wonders, and Church Growth" course at Fuller Theological Seminary experienced a breakthrough from their environment. When they saw the miracles taking place in the classroom, their theology had to change.

No, God has not changed. The God we serve is a miracle-working God Who has always dealt with His people by performing miracles on their behalf.

Why would God stop working miracles upon the Earth for thousands of years from the days of the New Testament Church and then before He returns show signs and wonders as promised in Matthew 24:29?

If God intended to stop performing miracles in the Church and in the lives of His people, why would He give the Church His miracle-working power? (Mark 16:17-18.)

Why would He tell us that signs and miracles – supernatural occurrences which cannot happen by human means, such as healings and deliverance – would follow believers?

To say that God has stopped performing miracles, or that "miracles aren't for today" is equivalent to saying that God has ceased to function as God – that He doesn't hear and answer prayer.

If you have been hindered by your environment, your theology, what you have heard others say regarding miracles, there is no better time than the present to ask God to help you break through your environment. Do not allow the traditions of man or any preconceived ideas to hinder you from receiving the miracle you need.

Decide for yourself. You cannot live your life based on what someone else believes.

Will the God Who created the heavens and the Earth (Genesis 1:1) – the God Who brought the children of Israel out of Egyptian captivity and provided food and clothing for them 40 years in the wilderness

(Deuteronomy 8:2-4) – the God Who sent His Holy Son into the world to die to set men free from the power of sin, sickness, and death (John 3:16-17) – the God Who resurrected Christ from the dead (Acts 2:31-32) – the God Who gave spiritual gifts, power and authority to the believer (I Corinthians 12:4-6, Luke 10:19) – the God Who will one day soon set up His heavenly kingdom on Earth (Revelation 21:3) – work a miracle for you?

Yes, He will. He has performed miracles for me and thousands of others around the world. He will do the same for you.

Does God Perform Miracles To Prove Himself?

As I stated earlier, man is a product of his environment. Because he has been taught that miracles are not for today, he probably is not familiar with the supernatural power of God, and he makes excuses. He tries to explain away miracles or refers to them as "Satan's counterfeits."

There are ministers today who have taught people for years that God doesn't perform miracles to prove Himself and that miracles are a carnal ministry.*

What about you? What do you think?

Have you ever given much thought concerning the importance of miracles? If you are the average person, you probably haven't. If you have witnessed a miracle, or have heard about someone else who has experienced a miracle, you have probably rejoiced and given thanks to God for it. Somehow, just the fact that a miracle has happened seems to be sufficient.

However, if you are to have a breakthrough in your personal environment, and raise your level of expectation to the point where you are expecting miracles to happen to you on a consistent basis, it is very important for you to understand the importance of miracles today.

Basically, God has two purposes for performing miracles:

1. To fulfill His Will and confirm His Word; and
2. To provide for the needs of His people.

On many occasions, God has used miracles to prove Himself.

There were many gods in the Old Testament. Every heathen tribe had their gods. But, their gods were carved out of wood and stone. Their gods could not see…they could not hear.. they could not speak.

God proved to the world that He was the only true and living God. How did He do it? Through miracles and through divine, supernatural interventions in the lives of the Jewish people, God raised up a people and manifested Himself to the world through those people, so that the whole world would know there is only one God – the true God, the *living* God – and Jehovah is His Name.

To illustrate, let's use Moses as an example. God called Moses and gave him a special job to fulfill. Moses was chosen by God to lead the children of Israel out of Egyptian bondage.

The job of leading millions of Jews out of Egypt was an impossible task in the eyes of Moses, but God had a plan. He was not only going to use miracles to lead the Jews out of Egyptian bondage, He was also going to use miracles to reveal Himself for the first time to His people as JEHOVAH. They knew Him by the name of God Almighty, but now they were going to know Him as Jehovah – their Deliverer, Provider, Healer.

God revealed to Moses how He would use miracles to fulfill His Will and His Word. He had entered into a solemn covenant with Abraham, Isaac, and Jacob. God had promised to give their descendants the land of Canaan. He had heard the groanings of the people of Israel who were in slavery to the Egyptians, and now the time had come. He was ready to deliver them.

To further emphasize to the people of Israel how important a visible manifestation of the fulfillment of His Word to them was, God hardened

Pharaoh's heart nine times so that He would have more opportunities to prove to Israel and Egypt His great miracle power. It was not until after God had turned the water of Egypt into blood (Exodus 7:19-20); sent plagues of frogs, lice, flies, boils, hail, locusts, and the plague on the cattle (Exodus, Chapters 8-10); sent darkness throughout Egypt for three days (Exodus 10:21-22); and killed all the firstborn throughout Egypt (Exodus 12:29) that Pharaoh released the Israelites. God used all these miracles to fulfill His Word and His Will.

All throughout the Old Testament Jehovah God proved Himself. He was the God Who led the children of Israel in a pillar of cloud by day and a pillar of fire by night. Who answered by fire. Who rolled back the Red Sea. Who stopped the mouths of lions and quenched the violence of fire that caused the heathen to say, "There is no god like unto the God of Israel."

God also used miracles to reveal Himself in the New Testament. When Jesus was here on Earth, He went everywhere preaching, teaching, and performing miracles.

The Bible also makes it very clear why great multitudes of people followed Jesus. They followed Him because blind eyes opened, and deaf ears unstopped, they saw the lame walk.

Through miracles Jesus revealed Himself as the Son of God, the promised Savior. When the forerunner of Christ, John the Baptist, was in prison, he sent two of his disciples to ask Jesus if He was the promised Messiah (Matthew 11:2-3).

Jesus answered by telling them to go tell John that the blind receive their sight, and the lame walk, the lepers are cleansed, and the deaf hear, the dead are raised up, and the poor have the gospel preached to them (Matthew 11:4-5).

He pointed to the miracles as proof of Who He was.

On another occasion when the Jews were ready to stone Him, He referred again to the miracles or works He had done.

If I do not the works of my Father, believe me not. But if l do, though ye believe not me, believe the works: that ye may know, and believe, that the Father is in me, and I in him (John 10:37-38).

God used miracles to prove Himself and to fulfill His Word and Will throughout the Old and New Testaments, and He is still doing the same today wherever people will open their hearts to believe and receive.

Another very important purpose for God performing miracles today is to provide for the needs of His people.

I would like to share two examples, one from the Old Testament and one from the New Testament, that illustrate God meeting people at the point of their need by performing a miracle on their behalf.

In the Old Testament, there was a little widow woman who had a great need (II Kings 4:1-7). Her husband died, leaving her with a large debt. She had no one to turn to, no means of satisfying her creditor. In fact, the man she owed money to had threatened to take her two sons as his servants to settle the debt. The only thing she possessed of value was a small bottle of oil.

She didn't know what to do but she knew a prophet of God named Elisha. She went to him and explained her problem.

What do you think Elisha did? He didn't look to himself or to man for the answer. He didn't ask God if it was His Will to meet this woman's need. He knew God and trusted Him for a miracle.

Elisha's instructions were simple enough. He told her to go borrow as many empty containers as she could find. Then she was to shut herself up in her house with her two sons and begin to pour the oil out of the small bottle into all the empty containers.

In the natural, what Elisha asked her to do seemed ridiculous but she did not question him. She was obedient. She recognized Elisha as God's spokesman and acted on his word. This action required a simplicity of faith in God and in the prophet of God.

Many people have difficulty in reaching this point because they are too busy trying to reason things out for themselves.

As a result of her simple act of obedience, having had and faith in the word spoken by the prophet, she received a miracle.

God supernaturally multiplied the oil until all the containers she had borrowed were filled. She sold enough to pay the debt she owed and had the rest to live on.

Another good example of a miracle being performed to meet a need is the problem a woman faced in the New Testament. It is easy to identify with her need because at one time or another most people suffer some type of sickness.

This woman had suffered from a flow of blood for 12 long years. She had tried everything. Her money was gone. Instead of her condition improving, it only grew worse.

One day she heard about a Man who had power to heal. She was desperate. This was her last hope. She believed and acted upon the word that she had received.

She did not allow anything to stand in her way. Gone was her pride, her fear of what others would think. She was willing to face the criticism and rejection of the crowd. She pushed her way through to Jesus.

There was no one there to tell her that she was unworthy to receive a miracle. There was no one there to tell her that following after miracles was carnal. She came to Jesus *expecting* to receive. There was no doubt, about if it was God's Will. She knew that if she could even touch His clothing, she would be healed. In response to her need and her simple faith in the Living Word, she received a miracle from God.

There are many more examples in the Bible where God performed miracles to meet needs, but what is so exciting to see today is that God is still meeting people at the point of their needs. I have hundreds of letters on file of people who had a need, cried out to God, and received the miracle they needed.

There is no doubt in my mind that God still works today. No one could change my mind because I have experienced God's miracle power many, many times.

So, you see, in God's relationship to man, miracles are extremely important. They are not carnal manifestations for the fulfillment of the flesh. Their purpose is to provide for the needs of God's people and to fulfill His Word and Will on Earth.

Will God Meet Me At The Point Of My Need And Perform A Miracle For Me Today?

After you understand clearly what a miracle is, the purpose for miracles begin to break through your personal environment and raise your level of expectancy. You will see that in God's total plan and purpose for you, He planned that miracles be part of your life.

Most people have mistakenly relegated miracles to a happening, a once-in-a-lifetime experience. Don't fall into that trap. Miracles are the natural characteristic of God and should also be part of our nature.

You were made for miracles!

Man is a miracle creation of God. You were created for miracles and miracles were created for you.

Miracles are not the exception. God's purpose for your life is that you live, breathe, and move in the supernatural.

God spoke the world into existence.
He said, ***Let there be light*** and there was light.

His words brought miracle after miracle – the sun, moon, stars, the sea, the heavens, trees, flowers, birds, fish – every ***living*** thing that you see on Earth today is a miracle of God.

From a little pile of dust He formed man and breathed the breath of life into him.

God placed Adam and Eve upon the Earth and provided everything they needed. He planned for them to live a miracle existence. He intended for them to never die. They were free of worry, pain, or disease.

He placed them in a beautiful garden with fruit and herbs of every kind. They didn't need any clothing to protect them from the elements of the weather, because He created a perfect temperature for them.

Not only did He create everything by a miracle, and provide everything Adam and Eve needed to survive, He fellowshipped with them. They were His creation, and He treated them as His children. In the cool of the day He came down to the Earth. He walked and talked with them.

This was God's original plan for man. God's intention was total care, total provision.

This idyllic setting is far removed from our lives today. We live in a world filled with pain, sorrow, turmoil, fear, confusion, hate, war, strife, sin, disease, and death. Man struggles to exist. We strive to earn enough money to provide even the basic necessities of life. Our bodies grow tired and old. We suffer the effects of a wide range of sicknesses, from a mild cold to terminal diseases such as cancer or heart disease.

All of these things were not part of God's original plan. Because of Adam and Eve's disobedience, we now are confronted with the problems and conditions that exist as a result of their sin against God.

God has made *miracle provisions* for you. Even though you live in this type of environment, it is possible for you to have every need in your life met on a consistent basis. He wants you to live in a rhythm of miracles, where miracles are a normal part of your life.

God has provided a way for you through the life, death, and resurrection of His Son, Jesus Christ, to have access to Him (Romans 5:1) – where all things are possible (Matthew 19:26) – where all your needs can be met (Philippians 4:19) – and where you can receive anything simply by asking in Jesus' Name (John 14:13).

God wants you to live in a rhythm of miracles! How is all this possible? Through a miracle-working God Who has made *miracle provisions* for you in His Word.

Remember the definition of a miracle – something which cannot happen by human means.

And the purpose of miracles today – is to provide for your needs and to fullfill God's Word and His Will.

God's Word is full of promises to you which require a miracle, a divine intervention, something which cannot happen by human means. He would not have given you so many promises requiring a miracle if He did not intend for you to experience miracles on a regular basis.

In the next few chapters, I will be sharing with you five steps which will help you receive a miracle and help you live in a rhythm of miracles where miracles are a normal part of your life.

These steps are found in the events that transpired in the life of Elisha, the children of Israel, and four poor, doomed lepers (II Kings 6:24-33, 7:1-20). It was a time of hopelessness, or a time of miracles. There was nothing that could be done by human means to change the situation.

But before we take the first step, I want you to see and identify with the great need that was present in the lives of God's people. The King of Syria came to Samaria and besieged the city until there was a great famine. Unusual things began to happen. The people began to do things they normally wouldn't do, and eat things they normally wouldn't eat.

The Bible says that an ass's head was sold for fourscore pieces of silver, and a cab of dove's dung was sold for five pieces of silver. The condition was drastic. But that wasn't all. The condition became so desperate, the famine so severe, that they resorted to cannibalism. They boiled children and ate them.

Throughout the next few chapters, as we refer to this very great need – and the great miracle that occurred in the life of Elisha, the children of Israel, and the four lepers – I want you to make it more personal and relative to you by inserting the problem or circumstance that you are facing right now that needs a divine intervention of God.

Whatever your problem may be, if you need a solution that cannot be met by human means, you need a miracle.

Are there habits in your life or in the life of someone you love – alcoholism, drugs, overeating, smoking – that have caused you pain and heartache, yet you feel powerless to overcome them? You may have tried every human means possible to change these circumstances, but nothing seems to help. *Get ready for a miracle!*

Have the pressures on your job been building within you, causing you to have sleepless nights, and days filled with fear and anxiety? Every method you may have tried in order to find peace has only added to your frustration. You feel you are at a dead end. *Get ready for a miracle!*

In your marriage, love relationships may have died. Instead of love, there is unfaithfulness, bitterness, strife, unforgiveness. You have given up hope and are preparing to get a divorce. ***Get ready for a miracle!***

Your heart may be broken by rebellious children who are determined to discard the values you have taught them and go their own way. You walk the floors at night wondering where they are and what trouble they are in. You have tried every means available to you. You have reasoned, pleaded, and applied every psychological technique with no results. ***Get ready for a miracle!***

In your finances, you may have hit rock bottom. Week after week there is not enough money to go around, to put food on the table, to buy clothes for your children, to make repairs on your house and car. There seems to be no help in sight and no way out. ***Get ready for a miracle!***

Physically you may feel you have gone as far as you can go. You have made endless visits to the doctor and were give medication, therapy, or surgery… and yet, your condition remains unchanged. The pain is there as a constant reminder. ***Get ready for a miracle!***

[1]Reprinted by permission from Christian Life magazine, copyright October 1982, Christian Life Missions, Wheaton, Illinois 60188.

The Miracle Book

Chapter Two

Step 1
See God As He Is

God is bigger than your need. He is greater than all the problems of every person on this Earth combined.

God is greater than all the existing problems that the nations of this Earth face today. He is greater than the economic disasters.

His power is greater than all the nuclear weapons man could ever create.

With just one word spoken by God, all the fighting and wars among the countries and nations of our world would come to a halt. Peace would reign upon the Earth. He has that power.

One word spoken by God and all the empty, bloated bellies of the millions of children, men, and women around the world – who are suffering from malnutrition and are dying from starvation every minute – one word, and those empty bellies would be filled and their emaciated bodies restored to perfect health. Just one word!

One word from God and every person on the face of the earth who is suffering disease of every kind – cancer, heart disease, diabetes, arthritis, multiple sclerosis, emphysema – one word from God, and they would be instantly healed. Every crippled, twisted body would be straightened, and every blind eye would be opened. God could speak the word, and missing arms and legs would reappear, and new eyes and ears would be created.

It is possible. All things are possible with God (Mark 10:27).

In an instant God could speak the word, and all the hatred, all the evil imaginations of man's heart would be erased – no more murders, no more stealing, no more pornography, no more need for drugs or alcohol, and no more violence. One word, and love would fill the heart of every person alive today.

As sophisticated and advanced as man's thinking is today, even taking into consideration all the tremendous scientific discoveries and breakthroughs man has made throughout the years, his ability to think and reason is limited. He cannot begin to comprehend the vastness of God's ability.

You may be thinking, If God can speak a word bringing peace to the war-torn nations of this world, if He can solve all our economic and social problems, if He can feed the hungry and the poor, if He can restore health to those who are dying, why doesn't He do it? Why doesn't He speak the word?

I have news for you. He has already spoken the word that will one day restore peace, love, and complete harmony to the world.

What is that word?

It is all summed up in one powerful majestic Name: JESUS!

God has already spoken to every need that now exists or may exist in the future.

He has set in motion a plan that will eventually restore peace to the world. This plan also includes the establishment of a new kingdom upon this Earth, where there will be no sickness, no pain, no sorrow, and no death. God the Father will establish a new heaven and a new Earth. In this new heavenly kingdom, God will come down and live with us. We will see Him face to face and will live forever with Him.

Sound too good to be true? You can read about it in a word He spoke to man nearly 1900 years ago in the Bible, which is the written Word of God (Revelation 21:1-4).

If He has already spoken the word (and He has) why are the world's conditions growing worse by the day? Why haven't we seen significant changes?

The answer to those questions is the first step you must take toward receiving the miracle you need and having miracles happen in your life on a consistent basis.

You must see God as He is. He is all powerful, all knowing, everywhere present.

Men have failed to recognize God. They have failed to see Him as their Deliverer, their Provider, and their Healer. Most people who believe there is a God do not know Him as their heavenly Father Who loves and cares for them as a natural father cares for his children (Luke 12:6-7).

How Do You See God?

To most people, God is some unseen force up in the sky. They may believe He exists somewhere but feel He is distant, too hard to reach. People feel that if there is a God, He is too busy to be concerned about their day-to-day problems and needs.

Nothing could be farther from the truth. God is anxiously waiting to help anyone who calls upon Him. In His Word it says, *For the eyes of the LORD run to and fro throughout the whole earth, to show Himself strong on behalf of those whose heart is loyal to Him* (II Chronicles 16:9, New King James Version).

When a person is born into the Kingdom of God, He becomes a child of God. No longer is God some unseen, far-removed power in the sky somewhere. God becomes a loving Father.

God knows all about you and is waiting to meet your needs.
He knows your name (John 10:3).
He knows your thoughts (Psalm 139:2).

He knows every word you speak (Psalm 139:4).
He knows the steps that you take (Psalm 139:2-3).
He knows how frail you are (Psalm 103:14).
He knows how much you are able to bear (I Corinthians 10:13).
He knows what you need before you ask (Matthew 6:8).

But all too often, instead of looking to an all-powerful God and a loving heavenly Father for a solution, man has foolishly thought he has had all the right answers. The majority of the people in our world today choose to use their own limited resources and go their own way rather than depend upon God and go His way.

How do you relate to God?

In your relationship with Him, has He become closer to you than a brother? This is the relationship He wants you to develop with Him.

Have you been going to Him when you have a need or a problem, such as: loneliness, depression, fear, insecurity, pain, sickness, sorrow? Or, have you been looking to yourself and natural resources instead of His miracle provisions for you?

When God brings good things into your life – a loving wife or husband, the birth of a new baby, success in your career, financial security – do you recognize Him as the Giver of all good gifts (James 1:17) and thank Him for it? Or, do you attribute them to your own personal achievements?

If you have accepted Christ into your life, and have been born again, you have all the faith you need to come to Him. You already have the faith to receive the miracle you need.

It is that simple. Don't get hung up on man's theologies. Break out of your own personal environment. Begin to use the faith God has given you. Start by taking those little, insignificant things in your life that perhaps you thought God wasn't interested in. Release the faith God has given you, and believe Him to supernaturally intervene, to give you a miracle.

Faith is like a tiny seed that will grow larger and stronger the more you use it (Matthew 17:20). Generally speaking, an individual cannot expect to have strong faith to believe God to open blind eyes or heal cancer if he has not exercised and built his faith by believing God for the little things in his own life, such as a headache or a cold.

A person cannot believe God for a miracle of $5,000, $10,000, or $15,000 if he has not yet exercised his faith by believing God to supernaturally intervene concerning a smaller debt or need of $50 or $100.

Time and time again I have seen this happen in services I have held throughout the country. People who have not been exercising their faith and believing God for miracles in their daily life in the little things, come to a meeting expecting God to heal them from a much more serious physical, mental, or spiritual condition.

On occasions, God increases or gives an individual an extra amount of faith, beyond their normal faith, to believe God for a great miracle of healing or deliverance (either for themselves or for someone else), and a miracle happens.

Also, there have been cases where people with a very serious condition or disease – who have had little or no faith at all – instantly receive a miracle healing. God responded to their need and the faith of someone else. There is a beautiful illustration of this in the New Testament in Mark 2:1-12, the people had gathered together in a room to hear Jesus. The place was packed. From one wall to the other people were jammed together until there was no room to move.

There is a beautiful illustration of this in the New Testament. (Mark 2:1-12).

The people had gathered together in a room to hear Jesus. The place was packed. From one wall to the other people were jammed together until there was no room to move. Jesus was preaching the word to them when four men arrived, carrying a paralyzed man on a stretcher.

Because the crowd blocked the doorway, these men looked for another way in. They brought their paralyzed friend up on the roof. They proceeded to take the roof apart and lowered the man right down in front of Jesus. When Jesus saw the strong faith of these four men, he responded to meet the man's deepest needs. Jesus forgave his sins and healed his paralysis.

God always responds to faith, whether it is the personal faith of someone in need or the faith of someone else. When you use your faith for needs in your own life, then your faith will increase and grow stronger.

So, in taking the first step toward a rhythm of miracles, you must see God as He is. You cannot see or reach God through your natural senses, your intellect, or your good works. There is only one way.

You must surrender your will, and accept Jesus Christ. Then the sixth sense, called faith, and the Giver of faith Himself, the Author and Finisher of our faith (Hebrews 12:2), will live in you.

Faith now abides, and ***nothing is impossible!***

To see God, and receive His miracle provisions for your life, you must come to Him in and through the gift of faith He has now given you. You must believe that He is, and that He is a rewarder of those who diligently seek Him (Hebrews 11:6, James 1:6).

You do not need to struggle for the faith to reach God.
As you receive Christ into your life, you receive faith as a gift (Ephesians 2:8).

With these two basic truths (your acceptance of Jesus Christ and God's gift of faith) as a foundation, let us go farther in this very important first step of seeing God as He is.

God Is Not Limited By Time Or Space

In Chapter One, I described to you the desperate situation Elisha, the children of Israel, and four lepers faced – hunger, fear, frustration, a sense of hopelessness – during a great famine in Samaria. In this weakened position, people had resorted to inhuman practices in order to survive.

The king of Israel heard how mothers were conspiring with each other to boil and eat their children. He became so enraged at the condition, the king of Israel began to accuse God and Elisha, the prophet of God.

The king had a very limited vision of God. He did not see Him as the unlimited, all-powerful God of Abraham, Isaac, and Jacob.

The circumstances were so overwhelming that he forgot all the miracles God had performed for the nation of Israel as He led them out of Egyptian captivity.

It is easy for us to look at the king's actions and condemn him. How could anyone forget how God miraculously provided food for the nation of Israel by raining down manna for 40 years in the wilderness? (Manna was a small, round, white wafer, with the taste of honey, which they used to bake bread.) Was it so easy for the king to forget how God miraculously kept their clothes and shoes from wearing out?

Yes, we may condemn the king. But if we will be completely honest with ourselves, we can remember times when we all have faced our own desperate circumstances where, in one way or another, we have either forgotten God or have limited Him in some way in performing the miracle we need.

In those moments when the circumstances seem to overwhelm us, we do not see God in all His power. We do not deal with God as He is.

When a person is hospitalized, and learns that he has cancer and only has three or four months to live, it is difficult to look beyond the circumstances and see a supernatural God Who is not limited, Who has already provided a miracle provision of healing for him. Fear engulfs him and blinds him from seeing God as He is.

Day after day, when a mother is faced with the reality of caring for a severely disabled child, who needs constant attention, and there seems to be no progress, not even a ray of hope, it is difficult for her to look beyond those circumstances and see a loving, compassionate God, Whose creative powers are unlimited, and Who can and will restore that child to a perfectly normal body. The hard, cold facts that stare her in the face day after day limit her from seeing God as He is.

When a businessman sees his company crumbling and dissolving around him, when he has frantically searched for a way out by securing loan after loan, when he receives threatening letters of foreclosure on his business and home, when creditors are calling him on the phone, all of these circumstances fill him with a sense of hopelessness that hinders him from seeing the God Who can turn his impossible situation around.

Pain, fear, hopelessness, and the hard, cold facts all hinder people from seeing God as He is. This was the case with the king of Israel. In the pressure of the moment, when he was faced with the hopelessness of the situation, fear gripped his heart. He forgot the miracle-working God of his fathers and took matters into his own hands. The king had not learned to deal with God on a supernatural plane.

In my own personal life I have had the privilege of meeting and working with all different types of people and their personalities. God has given me a very great truth to help me in successfully dealing with these different personalities, and I believe it also applies to our relationship with God.

All success in life comes from dealing with people, places and things as they are and not as you would wish them to be.

If you want to be successful in dealing with a person, you must know where he is coming from. You must know what he thinks, what makes him as he is. You must understand him. Once you do, you can deal with him as he is.

The same is true with God. If you are going to be successful in dealing with God, you must have a clear understanding of Him. And when you understand that He is a supernatural God, and understand some of His characteristics and His ability, you will know that He is able to meet any and all circumstances you will ever face.

God is supernatural.

When you know God, you understand that there is absolutely nothing strange about supernaturalism, because the word "God" means "One who must be worshiped as having supernatural ability; the Supreme Being" – not "a" supreme being but "the" Supreme Being.

The word "supernatural" means "that which goes beyond the law and power of nature." God, Who is supernatural, can go beyond any law or power of nature.

God is not limited by the laws of nature. He created them.
If God has to, He can shut up the heavens (James 5:17).
If He has to, He can make axe heads to swim (II Kings 6:5-6).
If He has to, He can cause donkeys to talk (Numbers 22:28).

There is nothing too hard for God. How do you see and understand God?

You and I are limited by the law of gravity, God is not. You and I are limited to time and space, God is not.

God has the ability to be everywhere present all at one time. The same moment He is intervening in the circumstances in your life and meeting your need, He can also be performing miracles for millions upon millions of people around the world simultaneously.

God is a Spirit. He is in every country: Mexico, India, Brazil, Kenya, Russia, Malaysia, Germany, Australia. He is in every city: Hong Kong, London, Paris, New York, Miami, Los Angeles, Vancouver, Calgary, Toronto. He is everywhere present at the same time. He is with you wherever you are. He is with me as I pen these words right now!

God is the Supreme Being. "Supreme" means "highest in rank and power and authority."

In our world today there are great men and women – presidents, prime ministers, kings, queens, and other high-ranking officials – who possess a tremendous amount of political and military power. Their position of authority demands respect and obedience.

I can still remember how I felt when I met the President of Chile in Santiago. The bands were playing, and as I stepped out of the car, they rolled out a plush red carpet. The guards met me and took their place, one on each side, and they proceeded to escort me into the presence of the highest-ranking soldier, the leader of the land. (I have had this experience many times.) I realized that this man had absolute power and that every person in his country was required to be in submission to him. Every order must be obeyed.

If we were to combine all the power and authority of every national leader in the world, it would still not compare with the power, the authority, and the supremacy of God. He overrules and rules over all! He is God, highest in rank, authority, and power. He is supreme!

All power and authority in heaven and Earth is given to Jesus Christ (Matthew 28:18). Men today may not recognize or submit to His power and obey Him, but one day every knee shall bow down, and every tongue shall confess that Jesus Christ is Lord (Romans 14:11).

There are two individuals in the New Testament who came to Jesus with a great need. One had a limited vision of Jesus; the other saw Him as He is, the all-powerful Son of God.

One was a woman who had welcomed Jesus into her home on many occasions. She had listened as He taught others how to know God. She knew Christ very well and had become a devout follower. She had probably witnessed many miracles. Yet, when she faced a very great need in her life, she failed to see Jesus as He really is.

A little woman by the name of Martha had a need. Her brother had become very sick, and she had sent word for Jesus to come and heal him.

Jesus loved Martha. He also loved her sister, Mary, and her brother, Lazarus, very much. Yet, when He heard about Lazarus being sick, He did not go immediately to them.

Always remember that God's ways are not our ways (Isaiah 55:8-9). We must continue to trust Him completely when things do not happen the way we want them to. We must allow God to answer our prayers any way, any time, and any place He chooses.

Jesus knew that Lazarus had died before he left to go to the city of Bethany, where Martha, Mary and Lazarus lived. He also knew the power that God had given Him to raise the dead. He knew the power within Him was not limited. He had a purpose. He wanted to build their faith by raising Lazarus from the grave.

As Jesus was approaching the city, Martha ran out to meet Him. "If only You had been here, Lazarus would not have died." Things had certainly not worked out the way Martha had planned. She had sent for

Jesus hoping He would get there in time to heal Lazarus. Now Lazarus was dead.

Martha had no doubt heard stories and had seen miracles performed by Jesus. Among the miracle stories, it is possible she had heard how Jesus restored life to the widow's son in Nain (Luke 7:11-17), and how He raised a girl from the dead in the city of Capernaum (Mark 5:22-24, 35-43).

But now, faced with the reality that Lazarus had been dead for four days, she had given up hope. Oh, yes. She said she believed Jesus was the Son of God, and that Jesus could perform miracles, but she was not expecting Him to supernaturally intervene in this situation.

Jesus told her, Martha, let me tell you something. Your brother, Lazarus, is in the tomb, but he is coming out. Your brother is going to rise again.

Martha said, I know in the resurrection day he is coming out. She saw into the future, tomorrow, but failed to see the reality of the God of the now.

Jesus said, Take a good look at Me, Martha. I *am* the resurrection.

Martha knew Jesus had performed miracles in the past. She knew He could do it in the future, but what about the present? She had limited His miracle power to a specific time and condition. She believed Jesus could have healed Lazarus before he died, but now, after being dead for four days, what could Jesus do?

When they arrived at the place where Lazarus had been laid in a cave, Jesus commanded them to roll back the stone.

Still doubtful and unbelieving, with her eyes on the hard, cold facts, Martha said, But, Jesus, don't You know that by now his body has begun to decay and stinks? After all, it has been four days.

Martha was not the only one present who limited the miracle power that flowed through Jesus. Some of the mourners who had accompanied them to the tomb were standing by questioning, wondering why this Man called Jesus had allowed Lazarus to die. If He really had power to open blind eyes, why didn't He stop Lazarus from dying?

It seems there are always those who would rather question why than to put their eyes on a miracle-working God and trust Him for a mighty supernatural intervention of His power.

Their lack of faith troubled Jesus. He had a purpose to fulfill. He wanted to meet their needs and build their faith. He spoke the words, *Lazarus, come forth,* and Lazarus's spirit re-entered his dead body. He came out of the grave as living proof of God's unlimited ability.

There is also a miracle story in the New Testament that shows us a man who was able to take the limits off Christ and see Him as He is (Matthew 8:5-13). In all probability, this centurion at that time was not a follower of Jesus Christ. He was a Roman soldier, a captain in the army. His allegiance, his loyalty, was to Caesar, to Rome.

He also had a need. His servant was very sick with the palsy and was in great pain. He brought this need to Jesus. Jesus told him. "I will come and heal him."

The centurion looked at Jesus and said, Lord, take a good look at me. See these army bars? When I walk into the garrison, I say to one soldier, Go, and he goes; then I say to another one, Come, and he comes.

He said, Lord, I am a man of authority. When I speak, all of Rome stands behind me. When I look at you, I see something that goes beyond Rome. I see something that goes beyond the power of Caesar.

Jesus, don't come to my house. It is not necessary. All you have to do is stand right here and speak the word only, and my servant – who is many miles away, will get up out of his bed.

He is paralyzed, totally incapacitated; but if You will just speak the word, Lord Jesus, something will happen to his body, to his legs, and to every part of his being. He will rise up. He will get up off that bed.

If You will just speak the word, my servant will be healed. There is none higher in power, or in rank, or in authority than You, Jesus. Speak the word!

What this man actually was saying to Jesus was, *I see You as You really are. People are watching You perform great miracles. They really don't understand You, but I do. Act like who You are. Lord, speak the word!*

The need in the life of the Roman centurion's servant was tremendous. And, if the centurion had not seen Jesus as He is, as a Lord, that need might not have been met.

In our miracle story concerning the great famine in Israel, the king limited God. Like Martha, the existing conditions hindered him from seeing God as He is. Are your existing conditions so overwhelming that they hinder you from seeing God as He is?

Now, let's bring these illustrations closer to home. Concentrate for a moment on the need in your life. Which one of these illustrations do you identify with? Are you like Martha? Do you believe Christ had the ability and power to perform miracles in the past, and has the ability and power to work miracles in the future, but you are doubtful that He will perform a miracle for you today?

Or, are you like the Roman centurion? Do you see Jesus with all power, and all authority over every need and every problem in your life regardless of how difficult or impossible it may seem in the natural?

Can you look at your circumstance – sickness, depression, broken relationships, financial disaster – and say with complete assurance, "Lord, just speak the Word and go beyond my human limitations?"

Just speak the Word, and go beyond the laws of nature.

Just speak the Word, and I will receive the miracle I need.

Man is naturally limited. God is supernatural, unlimited, unchanging, ever present, and ever willing to meet your needs.

God is relevant to you at the point of your need. There is not a situation, there is not a problem, there is not a need that you face that is impossible with God.

Take every human limitation of time or space and cast it aside. Throw out any and all preconceived ideas how you desire God to meet your need. Deal with God as He is and not as you are, and you will be one step closer to a miracle.

The Miracle Book

Chapter Three

Step 2
Take Your Eyes
Off Your Circumstances

Oh, God, why did You allow this to happen to me? Don't You care about me any more? This burden is too hard to bear. Why me, God?

The moment tragedy strikes, the average person is gripped by a paralyzing fear. He acts on impulse. He panics. After the initial shock of what has happened subsides, to alleviate the pain and pressure of the moment, he tries to place the blame on someone else or upon God. Remember the story in Chapter Two about Martha's reaction to the death of her brother, Lazarus? She told Jesus, If You had been here, Lazarus wouldn't be dead.

Young couples who have lost a baby during childbirth struggle to find the answers, and finding none, many times they point their finger at God and say, Why did You take our baby? Why did You allow this to happen to us?

This is the point where the king of Israel found himself. A terrible tragedy had developed in his country. People were starving to death. They were at an all-time low. Fear gripped the king's heart. If something didn't happen soon, Samaria would be destroyed.

He kept his eyes upon the circumstances instead of taking this great need to a supernatural God. And the longer he kept his eyes on the existing conditions, the more he became enraged at the prophet of God. He began to accuse Elisha and blame God for the famine.

All the king could see was those mothers boiling children and the people eating donkeys' heads and doves' dung. All he could see was the misery and the trials they were going through. He forgot that he served the God Who created the heavens and the Earth!

In the heat of the moment and pressure of these circumstances, the king lashed out in anger. He tore his clothes and said, God do so and more also to me, if the head of Elisha the son of Shaphat shall stand on him this day! And he sent his messenger to kill Elisha.

Let's stop here a moment to look at this very traumatic time in the king's life and to consider his reactions to the circumstances he faced:

1. His eyes were on the circumstances;
2. He was fearful;
3. He blamed God and Elisha for the circumstances;
4. He was angry; and
5. He took matters into his own hands by sending a messenger to kill Elisha.

Now, let's go to Elisha's house to see his reactions. Before the king's messenger reached his house, God supernaturally revealed to Elisha that the king had sent someone to kill him (II Kings 6:32).

Not only was Elisha facing possible death due to the famine in Samaria, he also faced death at the hands of the king's messenger. How did Elisha respond to these circumstances?

Was he fearful, as most people would be under these circumstances? No, he wasn't. Why? Because his eyes were not on the famine or the king's messenger.

His eyes were on a supernatural God Who had multiplied the oil in one little container until it filled many pots and was sufficient to pay the debts of a little widow woman (II Kings 4:1-7).

His eyes were on a supernatural God Who had given an old barren woman a son, and when that son died, the same God had raised him from the dead (II Kings 4:8-37).

His eyes were on a supernatural God Who had multiplied 20 loaves of bread and a few ears of corn to feed a hundred men, with plenty to spare (II Kings 4:42-44).

His eyes were on a supernatural God Who had defied the laws of gravity and caused an axe head to swim (II Kings 6:1-7).

His eyes were on a supernatural God Who sent horses and chariots of fire to protect him from the king of Syria and his men who had surrounded him (II Kings 6:8-18).

Elisha knew the same God, Who had responded to all these other needs with a miracle, would do the same for him now. With the authority God had given him as a prophet, Elisha met his circumstances with a word from God.

He did not point his finger at God. He did not ask God why He had allowed these circumstances to come into his life. He did not wonder if it was God's will to deliver him and the people of Samaria.

He spoke the word, and God set in motion the events that would bring about a miracle. Elisha faced the terrible conditions of the famine. He faced the king's messenger, who came to cut off his head, by saying ... *Hear ye the word of the LORD; thus saith the LORD, Tomorrow about this time shall a measure of fine flour be sold for a shekel, and two measures of barley for a shekel, in the gate of Samaria* (II Kings 7:1).

Elisha did not panic. He was not fearful because he knew a miracle-working God, and his eyes were upon Him.

He knew how to face his circumstances. He knew there was a word from the Lord to meet this need.

You have seen the king's reaction to his circumstances, and you have seen how Elisha reacted to his circumstances. How do you react to the circumstances that come into your life?

When you face a tremendous challenge, which is beyond your capabilities, or when you face a situation that cannot be met by human means, how do you react? Are you immobilized by a fear that causes you to keep your eyes on your problems?

When your son or daughter becomes involved with drugs and is gone for weeks at a time – you don't know where they are or what they are doing – do you find it difficult to stop worrying, to take your eyes off the circumstances and believe God for a miracle, a supernatural intervention, something which cannot happen by human means?

When your marriage is in trouble – your relationship with your husband or wife is not what it should be, there are barriers of unforgiveness and resentment between you – in your heart do you secretly blame your husband or wife? Do you become fearful that your relationship will never improve?

As long as you concentrate on your problems with your husband or wife, things will never change. In fact, they will grow worse. Those problems are hindering you from seeing God as He is.

But, when you take your eyes off those circumstances – your husband's drinking problem, your wife's habit of nagging, your husband's or wife's unfaithfulness, your lack of communication – and keep them on a God Who is unlimited, you will begin to see things change in your life and in the life of your husband or wife.

Your first step toward receiving a miracle and having miracles as a natural occurrence in your life is *to see God as He is.*

Now, you must take the second step.

Take Your Eyes Off Your Circumstances.

You may be facing a problem or may have a specific need in your life right now that has made you fearful. This is the day for you to take your eyes off that problem and put them on a miracle-working God.

Step 2—Take Your Eyes Off Your Circumstances

I am not suggesting that you ignore a problem that exists or that you run from the circumstances that you face. In this chapter and in Chapter Four, I am going to share how it is possible for you to face your problems head on without any fear.

You are going to learn more about the two forces behind your circumstances:

1. How Satan wants to use your circumstances to defeat you and to accuse God; and
2. How God wants to intervene in your circumstances – to meet you at the point of your need – and give you a miracle.

I realize it is much easier for me to tell you to take your eyes off your problems than it is to place myself in your position facing your circumstances day after day.

I also realize it is not easy for a person to be confined to a bed or wheelchair or to be in constant pain and still be able to take his eyes off his circumstances.

But, it is possible. I know because there have been times in my life when I have been in pain, my wife at the point of death, not enough money to buy groceries, my life in danger, etc. Yet, through all of these experiences, God has taught me how and has enabled me to keep my eyes off my circumstances.

There is one very special experience in my life when I was facing a tremendous challenge which was beyond my capabilities.

I didn't know how I was going to meet this challenge, but God spoke to me with some very special words of encouragement. Later I had these words mounted on a plaque to share with those who need a miracle. These words have changed my life and have been an encouragement to thousands of others. I believe they will help you, too.*

For many years I had been going to the four corners of the Earth conducting mass overseas crusades. I saw thousands upon thousands receive Christ and miracles too numerous to count take place as I ministered. Blind eyes were opened. The deaf and mute were able to hear and speak. People discarded their crutches. They got up out of their wheelchairs, healed by the power of God.

As I traveled throughout the nations of the world, I also had seen the overwhelming needs of the people. I had seen their poverty, pain, disease, hunger, and their hopelessness. I knew there were multiplied thousands, even millions of people that neither I nor the missionaries could ever reach.

I realized there were countries that were being closed to missionaries and evangelists. God showed me that the key to a closing world was the Nationals…Africans reaching Africans. Chinese reaching Chinese. South Americans reaching South Americans.

In a very unforgettable experience in Porto Alegre, Brazil, in 1962, God gave me a commission. He said, "Son, Build Me an Army."

When I began to think about the doubling and redoubling of the world's population, and the tremendous challenge to build God an Army that would be able to reach the world in this generation, it was overwhelming.

I told God, "How can I do it? I'm only one man. I don't have a big television ministry to raise up millions of partners."

I will never forget that moment. I was in prayer in my hotel room prior to a seminar I was holding in Washington, D.C., when God literally spoke to my heart with these words:

> ** DON'T LOOK TO THE BIGNESS OF YOUR*
> *NEED. Look to the bigness of your God! Your*
> *circumstances are hindrances to seeing*
> *MY ABILITIES.*
> *If you keep your eyes on your circumstances, the devil will*
> *use your circumstances to defeat you and accuse the Word*

Step 2–Take Your Eyes Off Your Circumstances

of God, the written and the Living Word. Your VICTORY
is in keeping your eyes on the BIGNESS of your GOD
and His ABILITY. He has promised to take you STEP by
STEP by STEP – not all at once but step by step – AND
EACH STEP WILL BE A MIRACLE!

In all my ministry, nothing has strengthened me more than the comfort and constant daily guidance I receive as I repeat these miracle words over and over again.

Whatever your problem is right now – a domestic problem, a financial need, a sickness unto death – whatever that circumstance is, determine not to allow that circumstance to defeat you. Your victory will come as you keep your eyes on the bigness of your God, and He will lead you step by step, and each step will be a miracle.

Who Is In Control Of The Circumstances In Your Life?

Some people believe circumstances and events come into their life by chance. I don't!

If something bad happens to an individual: he loses his job, is involved in a car accident, or his wife leaves him, people call it a "bad break" or consider it a matter of "bad luck." On the other hand, when something good happens in life, such as: a promotion on the job, receiving an unexpected sum of money, meeting the right person and falling in love, making the right connection in a business deal, then people consider themselves fortunate and attribute these circumstances to "good luck."

Think back for a moment on the good and bad circumstances you have faced in your life. Did you attribute them to luck or chance? Did you give God the credit for the good? Did you blame God for the bad circumstances, you faced? Or, maybe at the time you faced the circumstances you simply accepted them as fate and didn't give any consideration to their source?

The circumstances that come into your life are not by chance. If you are born again and walking in obedience to God, you are considered righteous in His eyes, and the Word of God says that your steps are *ordered by the LORD* (Psalm 37:23).

That may be hard for you to understand, especially if you have recently experienced tragedy and heartache in your life. But once you understand that there are actually two forces at work in the circumstances in your life, and learn how to see beyond the circumstance and determine who is in control, you will not be fearful, and you will be able to take your eyes off your circumstances.

Have you ever known anyone who has experienced a tragedy in their life and has pointed their finger at the devil and blamed him for it? Why is it most people blame God? Is it because they believe God is in total control of events that take place in their life and therefore blame Him for allowing tragedies to happen? Or, is it because they fail to acknowledge that Satan is also at work in their circumstances?

What do you think? Does God send pain, sickness, and tragedy into the lives of His children?

The Bible is very clear on this subject. God is totally good. There is no evil in Him. He does not tempt man (James 1:13).

God does not send problems. He does not send financial disasters. He does not cause a marriage to break up. He does not send pain or sickness. He does not bring death and destruction.

God cannot operate contrarily to His Word.

God sent His Son, Jesus Christ, into the world that you might have life and have it more abundantly (John 10:10).

It is through Jesus Christ that you have been given miracle provisions which will restore you to that abundant life. (I will share more about these miracle provisions and how you can have them in Chapter Five.)

There are times when God will allow certain circumstances to come into your life to build and test your faith, to bring you into a new spiritual maturity. But, He will never allow any circumstance, any problem, to come into your life greater than what you are able to bear (I Corinthians 10:13). And, when those circumstances come, He will not leave you but will during the battle provide the solution. No battle, no solution. A battle always results in a solution, a great victory…a miracle! Recognize God is *always* in control.

Say it right now as you read this book:

"I am a child of God. Therefore, God is in total control of all the circumstances of my life."

There are no circumstances that Satan can bring into your life that can separate you from God or His love.

Who shall separate us from the love of Christ? shall tribulation, or distress, or persecution, or famine, or nakedness, or peril, or sword? Nay, in all these things we are more than conquerors through him that loved us (Romans 8:35,37).

If Satan, the enemy of your soul, has brought pain, sickness, distress, or financial problems into your life, know this:

The eyes of the LORD are upon the righteous, and his ears are open unto their cry (Psalm 34:15).

*The righteous cry, and the LORD heareth, and delivereth them out of **all** their troubles* (Psalm 34:17).

*Many are the afflictions of the righteous: but the LORD delivereth him out of them **all*** (Psalm 34:19).

*The LORD redeemeth the soul of his servants: and **none** of them that trust in him shall be desolate* (Psalm 34:22).

God is going to meet you at the point of your need. He will supernaturally intervene and deliver you out of your circumstance.

Always remember, God is in control of the circumstances in your life, not Satan, not anything evil.

Actually, as a Christian, you have an unfair advantage on Satan. Satan doesn't know your plans or your future. He cannot read your mind, but you can know his, because the Spirit of God within you will reveal his plans and prepare you for his attacks, just as God revealed to Elisha the king's plan to kill him (II Kings 6:32). There is not one thing that the enemy can do to you that God does not know about.

When Satan comes against you in your circumstances, keep your faith in God. Use the weapons of warfare He has provided, and know that God will give you victory.

Satan Tries To Use Your Circumstances To Defeat You

Not only is God there at the point of your need to work on your behalf and give you a miracle, Satan is also there to hinder you. Satan knows if he can get you to keep your eyes on the problem and not let you see the solution God has for you, the circumstances will be too big for you. This is one reason why so many people give up and live lives of defeat, despair, and utter frustration. With their eyes on their problems, they rely on their natural resources instead of believing God to supernaturally intervene and deliver them.

Some people make a very big mistake by not acknowledging the existence of the evil forces affecting their circumstances. They do not acknowledge the enemy of their soul. To them, the devil is just a "bogey man" they heard about as a child in Sunday School. They do not have a clear concept of him or his power, and they do not understand how he is involved in the circumstances in their life. He is just a red cartoon character with two horns, a pointed tail, and a pitchfork who is confined to a place of torment called hell.

Satan is not the figment of someone's imagination. He is real. In God's Word he is called "the destroyer", because his purpose is to destroy (Revelation 9:11). He is not confined to hell, but he is walking throughout the Earth today, and his purpose is to kill, steal, and destroy (I Peter 5:8).

Do not allow anyone to mislead you. Make no mistake about it. When you are born again, all of your problems do not disappear. You begin a new warfare, a spiritual warfare, where your struggle is not primarily with a person, a habit, or the cares of this world, although these things may be involved in your struggles.

This warfare is not with flesh and blood. It is spiritual warfare...*against principalities, against powers, against the rulers of the darkness of this world, against spiritual wickedness in high places* (Ephesians 6:12).

It is important that you know how the enemy works and the extent of his power, so when he attacks you through your circumstances, you will not be afraid, you will not accuse God, and you will not keep your eyes on your circumstances.

Satan is defeated and has no power over you except what you allow him to have. You are actually carrying on a spiritual warfare with an enemy who has already been defeated!

Through the life, death, and resurrection of Jesus Christ, Satan has been defeated in your life.

His blood has set you free from sin (Hebrews 9:14).

By his stripes you are healed (Isaiah 53:5, Matthew 8:17).

You have eternal life (I John 5;1 1).

You have power over all the enemy (Luke 10:19).

Since Satan is already defeated, where does the struggle (the bitter conflict) begin?

Using his power of deception, Satan comes to you at the point of your need. He doesn't want you to be victorious in your circumstances. He doesn't want you to have a miracle.

Satan will try to fill your heart with fear. He will tell you that you are defeated, that he is in control of your circumstances. He will try to use the circumstances in your life to accuse God.

Satan knows that if he can get you to keep your eyes on your problem, and not on a supernatural God, you will be defeated.

Think about it for a moment. In the problem or circumstance you are facing right now, have you entertained thoughts in your mind that your situation is hopeless or that you don't have enough faith to receive your healing or the miracle you need?

If you have never recognized it before, that is Satan putting those thoughts into your mind.

He will tell you that God is responsible for your circumstances. He will try to convince you that healing is not for today, that you are better off trusting doctors than trusting God.

He will bring financial problems into your life, and then he will tell you, See what happens when you trust God? All these years you have been faithful in paying your tithes, what good has it done? God is not interested in meeting your financial needs. You might as well accept these problems. There is nothing you can do. This is God's Will for your life.

Don't let Satan intimidate you. Stand firm in the knowledge that God has not changed. He can still roll back the Red Sea. God can still send manna from heaven to provide for His children. He can and will do whatever is necessary to deliver you and make you victorious. This is "God's Social Security System."

Turn Your Back On Unbelief

As you take the second step to your miracle by *taking your eyes off your circumstances,* you must also be ready to know how to deal with the negative forces of unbelief.

Begin to see God as He is the moment you take your eyes off your circumstances, and begin to expect a miracle in your life, you will be surrounded by those who will think that you've gone off the deep end. They will try to reason with you. They will make fun. They will criticize you.

Remember where we left Elisha and the king of Israel? They were on the doorstep of Elisha's house (II Kings 6:33). The king, his messenger, and his right-hand man were there to kill Elisha. Elisha had just met his circumstances head on with a word from the Lord. He told them that the very next day flour and barley would be sold at the gate of the city.

A word came from God to meet the circumstance. It did not come out of heaven. God did not speak it in a loud voice to all the people, but He used His prophet.

The word of the Lord came to Elisha. He stood up – facing the circumstance, facing those who accused God – and prophesied a blessing. He told them that within 24 hours God was going to supernaturally intervene in their circumstances. It was time for a miracle!
What was the reaction to this great announcement? Relief? Joy? Expectancy?

No, on the contrary. This word – that would bring a miracle to the people of Samaria – was met by unbelief and ridicule.

The king's right-hand man answered Elisha by saying, ...*If the Lord would make windows in heaven, could this thing be...*(II Kings 7:2, AMP). He mocked him. How could this possibly happen? The city had been besieged by Syria for a long time. There was no way humanly possible for this to happen.

Elisha was not moved by this man's ridicule. He didn't argue with him. He simply said, All right. You're going to see it with your eyes, but you're not going to eat it. What I spoke will come to pass. God will receive glory, but you'll never eat it.

I cannot think of anything more tragic than for a person to be surrounded by the manifestation of God's miracle power, yet not being able to enjoy it because of unbelief.

Put yourself in Elisha's place. Let's suppose the circumstance you are facing is a great financial need. Your husband has been unemployed for six months. You have no income and only enough food to last a few days. The children are starting to complain about being hungry. One day, during prayer, God quickens the Word: *But my God shall supply all your need according to his riches in glory by Christ Jesus* (Philippians 4:19).

You receive this word from God. You receive a spiritual breakthrough to visualize the riches of Christ in glory, and that Christ applies them to meet your needs. You realize that the same God Who provided for the needs of the children of Israel has not changed. He will do the same for you and your family.

God fills your heart with a spirit of expectancy and you cannot wait to share with your family what God has spoken to your heart.

As you gather around the table that night to share your meager rations of food, you excitedly tell your husband and children how God has promised that He is going to miraculously put food on your table.

Can you hear the reactions? Your husband pats you on the shoulder, What you say sounds great, honey. But we must be realistic. There is nothing left in the cupboards. We don't have any money and we don't know anyone who can lend us any. I'm not trying to discourage you but those are the cold hard facts. I have looked everywhere for a job. Why, only today I offered to wash dishes or wait on tables, but there were no openings.

The next day goes by, and you are still holding on to the promise God has given you that He will supply your needs. Your empty stomach is a constant reminder of your circumstances. Your children have been coming to you throughout the day asking you for something to eat. Your husband watches you as you set the table for dinner wondering if you have gone off the deep end. Why are you setting the table? Aren't you being a little silly? Aren't you carrying this a little too far? The children will laugh at you when they see you setting the table when there is no food.

Suddenly, the door bell rings, and there at the door is someone whom you haven't seen in a long time, who is unaware of your circumstances. In his arms he is carrying two bags full of groceries that God has told him to bring to your house.

When you refuse to listen to the negative forces that surround you, and instead keep your eyes on God and His ability, your prayers may not always be answered the way you expect them to be answered, but God will open up the windows of heaven if necessary to meet your need. God will provide manna from heaven to keep His promised Word.

When you step out in faith to expect a miracle, there are going to be those who will try to persuade you that you are acting foolishly. You must be persistent.

There was a blind beggar by the name of Bartimaeus who heard that Jesus was passing by, so he cried out in a loud voice, *Jesus, thou son of David, have mercy on me.* His faith and perseverance were rewarded, as Jesus touched him and opened his blind eyes (Mark 10:46-52).

Blind Bartimaeus did not listen to the negative voices of the crowd. If he had, he would not have received his miracle.

How did Jesus react to the negative forces He faced?

One day a ruler of the synagogue by the name of Jairus came to Jesus and told Him that his daughter was dying. Jesus responded to this need by telling Jairus, I will come and heal her.

But on the way to Jairus's house, Jesus was detained by the woman with the issue of blood, who pressed her way through the crowd, touched the hem of His garment, and was made whole.

By the time Jesus arrived at Jairus's house, the little girl was already dead. When they walked through the courtyard, all of the professional mourners were there. It was amazing how they stopped crying and started criticizing as Jesus and Jairus walked through the gate.

They said, Jairus, aren't you a ruler of the synagogue? What are you doing with that Healer?

If you had any love for your daughter, you would not have left her. Now look what happened. You've brought disgrace to your whole family. While you were out chasing the Miracle Worker, your daughter died.

How would you have faced this criticism and unbelief?

Jesus didn't say a word. He didn't say, Well, let Me prove to you Who I am. Let's go inside, and I will show you all the prophecies in the Old Testament about Me. He didn't put an ad in a newspaper and offer one thousand dollars for somebody to debate Him on a platform.

He just turned his back on their unbelief.

He said to Jairus, Let's not forget what I came here for. Come on, Jairus, let's get going.

Up the staircase they went until they came to the room where the little girl lay. She was dead. The cover was over her head. Jesus looked at Jairus and said, *Only believe*. He said to the girl, *Damsel ... arise*, and in one split second her spirit re-entered her body, and she jumped to her feet.

Jairus received a miracle because he turned his back on unbelief.

Don't forget that on your way to a miracle, you are going to hear many voices of unbelief.

Don't ever forget why God sent His Son, Jesus, into this world. *For this purpose the Son of God was manifested, that he might destroy the works of the devil* (I John 3:8).

Satan is going to try to use your circumstances to defeat you. He will try to keep your eyes on your circumstances. He will try to get you to blame God.

When he tries to fill your heart with fear, turn your back on him. Cast out the fear with the Word of God. Remember your authority. Speak the Word, the promises of God.

When others think you are foolish and try to discourage you from stepping out in faith to believe God for a miracle, turn your back on their unbelief, take your eyes off your circumstances, and keep right on walking. Each step will be a miracle.

Chapter Four

Step 3
See Your Problems As
Miracle Opportunities

There is a fool proof way for you to be able to face every circumstance in your life without being overcome by fear!

Once you fully understand that God wants to use your circumstances for your good – regardless of how difficult or trying they are – you will be able to have the same peace and the same confidence that Elisha possessed.

In our miracle story involving Elisha and the famine in Samaria, Elisha was able to look death squarely in the face and boldly speak forth the word God had given him concerning his need. He knew Satan was trying to use his circumstances to defeat him, but more importantly, Elisha knew that God was going to take those same circumstances, turn them around, and use them to His advantage.

Elisha did not see the great famine, and the possibility of his own death at the hands of the king's messenger, as a problem but rather as another opportunity for God to perform a miracle.

God rewarded Elisha's faith. He met Elisha at the point of his need. The all-knowing, all-powerful God of Elisha knew that the king had organized a plot to kill Elisha. A messenger was given instructions to knock on the door and when they opened the door, the messenger was going to seize Elisha and cut off his head.

God supernaturally revealed the plot of the enemy to Elisha while he was at home talking with the elders. Elisha said, *See ye how this son of a murderer hath sent to take away mine head? look, when the messenger cometh, shut the door, and hold him fast at the door: is not the sound of his master's feet behind him?* (II Kings 6:32).

Soon after Elisha had spoken these words, a knock came at the door. But before the messenger could lift his hand against Elisha, Elisha was given a word from the Lord to meet his circumstance.

That word changed Elisha's circumstance. That word saved Elisha's life and the lives of many others living during this great famine in Samaria. That word from God brought a miracle.

Remember, God's Word always comes forth to challenge our circumstances. There is not a problem, there is not a burden, there is not a circumstance that a simple loyalty in God's Word cannot change.

The third step toward your miracle is to *See Your Problems as Miracle Opportunities.*

In my life I have faced problems, trials, and test that could have made me fearful.

At Theresa's bedside, when she lay unconscious for three days and nights, had I not known that God was in control of our circumstances, I would have been fearful.

When the doctors told us our baby was dead, if we had not known that God was turning our circumstances around, Theresa and I would have been devastated. We would have given up hope.

Satan was using our circumstances to discourage me. He wanted me to accuse God for Theresa's sickness. He wanted me, as a husband and father and minister, to wonder if I was doing the right thing in trusting God.

There were instances in my life when I faced intense inner struggles, such as the time I was forced to leave Theresa at the point of death in a motel room and travel to another city in order to continue a crusade. I had confidence in God that He would take care of Theresa, but Satan put thoughts in my mind to discourage me. He whispered, "What kind of a husband are you to go off and leave your wife in such a condition? What will people think of you? You must not love your wife very much to leave her alone at a time like this."

It was during times like these that God would send His Word to comfort me. I knew God had promised to never leave nor forsake me (Hebrews 13:5). I knew that He had promised me that I would not be tested above what I was able to bear; but during the time of testing, He would provide a way of escape (I Corinthians 10:13).

I knew His Word said that all things were going to work for my good (Romans 8:28).

The Word of God sustained me in those discouraging circumstances and has continued to be my source of strength. I will be sharing more in Chapter Five about the potential that the Word has to bring you the miracle you need.

But first, let's "take off the mask." Let's once again take an honest look at the reactions most people have when a crisis or tragedy comes into their lives. In Chapter Three, we focused our attention on the initial reactions of shock and fear and how many people blame God for the bad circumstances that come into their lives.

How Do You React To Your Circumstances?

Think back for a moment to a time in your life when you faced a crisis situation or a deep need: sickness, broken relationships, separation, or financial disaster.

What did you feel?

Pain? Sorrow? Rejection? Anger? Resentment? Worry? Loneliness? What did you do?

If you are like most people, you probably found it was necessary to find some way and some place to release the emotions churning within you. You may have cried bitter tears, taken a long walk, searched for a quiet place to "sort things out," or looked for comfort from a friend.

These are the normal reactions, and there is nothing wrong with them. But, from my own personal experience, I have discovered it is far better to take your circumstances to God first. In this way, Satan will not be able to use your emotions to hinder you from receiving the miracle you need.

You see, if Satan can cause you to be fearful and filled with worry, anxiety, and self-pity, you will not be able to:

1. See God as He is;
2. Take your eyes off your circumstances; or
3. See your problems as miracle opportunities.

You must be on guard against these destructive emotions. Recognize them for what they are, a direct attack upon the faith God has given you.

All too often people become submerged in these negative emotions and may not even recognize it. They spend hours going over and over a problem in their mind. They cannot think of anything else. Worry so clouds their mind that it not only affects their thinking and their actions, it also affects their spirituality.

Worry is a sign that a problem has not been fully surrendered to the Lord. It also reveals a need to develop a greater trust in God and His ability.

God wants you to be free from fear, worry, and anxiety. He wants you to cast all your cares upon Him (I Peter 5:7).

He instructs you not to worry: *Don't worry about anything; instead, pray about everything; tell God your needs and don't forget to thank Him for His answers. If you do this you will experience God's peace, which is far more wonderful than the human mind can understand. His peace will keep your thoughts and your hearts quiet and at rest as you trust in Christ Jesus.* (Philippians 4:6-7, TLB)

He wants you to develop your trust in Him: *Trust in the LORD with all thine heart; and lean not unto thine own understanding. In all thy ways acknowledge him, and he shall direct thy paths.* (Proverbs 3:5-6)

Self-pity is another negative emotion that directly attacks your faith and will hinder you from seeing your problems as opportunities for God to work a miracle for you.

Have you ever noticed how defeated a person becomes when he constantly talks about his problems: his lack of money, his physical problems, his problems at work? When a person is overcome by self-pity and is constantly feeling sorry for himself, it is almost as if he has fallen into a deep, dark pit with no means of getting out.

Self-pity must be recognized and dealt with or it will turn into resentment against others and against God. This is the place Satan tries to keep most people, in the pit of self-pity and resentment.

Don't fall into his trap!

The moment tragedy or problems come into your life, don't allow Satan to have any opportunity to use your emotions against you. See God as He is. Keep your eyes off your circumstances. Trust Him, and expect Him to meet you at the point of your need with a miracle.

Earlier in this chapter we saw how Elisha faced his circumstances with courage, confidence, and a loyalty to God and His Word. Although the Bible does not give a detailed account of his reactions, I am sure he was not sitting around somewhere having a "pity party" and feeling sorry for himself.

I do not believe he was questioning God. I cannot imagine him reacting the way most people would. Oh, God, why did You allow this famine to happen to Your people? Why did you allow this to happen to me? You remember me, don't You, Lord? I'm Your prophet. I have been serving You faithfully all these years. Are You going to allow me to suffer and die with everyone else?

When God revealed to Elisha the enemy's plan to kill him, he didn't throw up his hands in despair and look for a place to hide. He had confidence in God and His miracle power.

Elisha was a man of prayer. No doubt he had spent many hours in prayer on behalf of the people and the terrible conditions they faced. He had called the elders together. It is even possible they had just finished a prayer meeting when the king's messenger knocked on the door.

When Elisha met his circumstances with a word from God, he did not just speak the first thing that came into his mind. That would have been presumptuous. But, because he had spent time alone with God in prayer seeking His direction, when the crisis came, he was ready. He had a prepared word from God!

Have you ever wondered why it is possible for some Christians to face any circumstance that comes their way with great wisdom and strength? If you could go "behind the scenes," you would be able to see the consistency of their daily communion with God, which prepares them for any problem they may face.

Too often people wait until the moment tragedy strikes to cry out to God. How much better it is to develop a good, strong, consistent relationship, so when Satan brings circumstances into your life to defeat you, you will be in a position where God can give you a word which will bring the miracle you need.

Step 3–See Your Problems As Miracle Opportunities

Do All Things Really Work Together For My Good?

When your life seems to be crumbling around you, and your heart is broken, it is hard to hear someone quote the scripture to you, *And we know that all that happens to us is working for our good if we love God and are fitting into His plans* (Romans 8:28, TLB).

In fact, you may secretly resent your friends telling you that all things are working together for your good.

You say to yourself:
How could they possibly say that? If only they really knew how I feel and what circumstances I am facing, they wouldn't say that.

The loss of a job, sickness, broken relationships, a pending divorce, financial disasters, how can any of these circumstances possibly work together for anyone's good? How can these bad circumstances most of us face at some time in our lives be even remotely connected with anything good?

Remember, Satan's objective is to use your circumstances to defeat you. His job is to steal, kill, and destroy. He is the one who brings divisions, sickness, and financial problems.

When you know God is not only going to make you victorious in the middle of your circumstances but will also use those same circumstances for your good, you will be able to face every circumstance without fear.

You will begin to develop an even greater trust in God and His miracle power.

You will be able to see your problems as miracle opportunities.

What do you think: Can God be trusted with the circumstances in your life? As God's child, are you aware that God is in control of *all* the circumstances in your life?

In the circumstances you are facing right now, are you worried and fearful, or are you trusting Him to work all things for your good?

From cover to cover, the Bible contains example after example of how God used circumstances for the good of all those who trusted in Him. If it were possible to ask some of the individuals who faced trying circumstances the question: Do you trust God with the circumstances in your life? – what do you think would be their response?

For example, let's ask a man who lost everything in one day:

His herd of oxen and asses were stolen and his servants murdered. Fire came out of heaven and consumed his sheep and the servants tending them. The Chaldeans stole his camels and killed his servants. While his seven sons and three daughters were having dinner in the eldest son's house, a great wind caused the house to collapse upon them, killing all of them.

On top of all these circumstances, he was stricken with boils from the top of his head to the bottom of his feet, and his friends and even his wife turned against him.

Imagine he is standing next to you, and you are questioning him.

What do you say, Job? Is it possible to trust God when all these terrible things are happening to you?

Job replies, *No matter what happens, though God slay me, yet will I trust in Him* (Job 13:15). *He knows all about me. He knows how much I am able to bear, and after my faith has been tested, I will come through victorious* (Job 23:10).

Job trusted God with his circumstances, and God was faithful. He healed Job's body, gave him seven more sons and three more daughters, and restored double his sheep, oxen, asses, and camels.

Step 3—See Your Problems As Miracle Opportunities

What about the Apostle Paul? What do you think he would say if he was asked if he trusted God with the circumstances of his life?

Paul, you have been beaten, shipwrecked, stoned, and left for dead. Can you still say that all things work together for good to those who love God? Without batting an eye, I can hear him say in a clear, forceful voice, ... *none of these things move me ...* (Acts 20:24).

. . . I was delivered out of the mouth of the lion. And the Lord shall deliver me from every evil work, and will preserve me unto His heavenly kingdom . . . (II Timothy 4:17-18)

For I am persuaded, that neither death, nor life, nor angels, nor principalities, nor powers, nor things present, nor things to come, Nor height, nor depth, nor any other creature, shall be able to separate us from the love of God, which is in Christ Jesus our Lord. (Romans 8:38-39)

Paul considered his adverse circumstances as "light afflictions" because he was not afraid. He saw God as He is. He believed God was in control and that everything happened in his life for a purpose.

He took his eyes off his circumstances.

He considered his problems only as another means for God to prove His miracle power.

Without any doubt whatsoever, I can say that regardless of who you are or the problem you face, if you will trust God, He will perform a miracle and use your circumstances to prove Himself strong on your behalf.

God Will Transform Your Problems Into Miracles

There is another clear example in the Bible of how God used circumstances as an opportunity to perform a miracle. It involves the events that happened in the life of a young 17-year-old boy.

As we look at his life, I want you to put yourself in his place. Compare his reactions with the way you would have reacted.

Joseph was the youngest of Jacob's sons and was greatly loved by his father. As a result, Joseph's brothers were jealous, and they hated him.

One day Joseph had a dream. In this dream, God revealed to him that He had a purpose and plan for his life and that one day he would be in a position of authority over his brothers and his entire family.

When Joseph shared his dream with his family, his brothers hated him even more. His father, who loved him dearly, rebuked him. How ridiculous! Why would they ever bow down before a little shepherd boy!

One day Joseph went out into the field to find his brothers. As he approached, they made plans to kill him. The oldest brother, Reuben, overheard their plans and talked them into sparing Joseph's life. They seized Joseph, tore off the coat his father had given him, and threw him into a deep pit.

For a moment, imagine you are in that pit with Joseph. It is dark and cold. There is no way of escape. There is no one to help. The only thing Joseph could cling to was the promise God had given him in a dream.

Can you identify with Joseph? Have you ever been in a position in your life where the circumstances were so bad that you felt like you were all alone in a dark, deep pit with no way out?

Perhaps God has given you a specific promise, or maybe He has placed a special calling upon your life, and Satan has placed obstacles and circumstances in your way in an effort to hinder you from receiving the fulfillment of that promise. Don't give up! Joseph didn't give up. He held onto his promise.

From that pit, Joseph was sold into slavery and taken into the land of Egypt.

How would you have reacted?

Most people would have become confused and afraid, maybe even a little doubtful that what God had promised would come to pass. All the outward appearances were discouraging, to say the least. It seemed as if God had forgotten all about Joseph. Why was God allowing him to be sold into Egyptian bondage?

Even though he had been betrayed by his own flesh and blood, was separated from his father and mother, and forced into slavery in a strange country, he did not feel sorry for himself. He was not resentful. He did not try to take matters into his own hands. He simply trusted God and held onto His promise. He saw his circumstances as an opportunity for God to work a miracle and fulfill His promise to him.

God was with Joseph and was using his circumstances for his good. Everything he did prospered, and he was given the position of overseer in the house of an officer of Pharaoh. Then, just when everything seemed to be going well, Joseph was falsely accused by his master's wife of trying to take advantage of her. He was bound and thrown into prison.

First a pit, then Egyptian slavery, and now prison! How would you have reacted to these circumstances?

Have you ever gone through difficult times until finally it seems God is beginning to pour out His blessings upon you, only to have another problem or tragedy arise? If you have, you can imagine how Joseph felt.

God was with Joseph in the prison and gave him favor with the keeper of the prison. Even in prison God caused Joseph to prosper! He did not give up hope. He held on to the promise he had received from God.

After two long years in prison, God brought Joseph out, and once again he was elevated to a position of power and authority. He was made second in command to the Pharaoh.

After 13 years, the promise God gave Joseph in a dream when he was 17 years old came to pass. Because of the famine that was in the land, Joseph's brothers were forced to come to Egypt to buy grain. They came and bowed down before him, just as God had shown him they would.

God did not take Joseph immediately out of his circumstances.

He made Joseph victorious in his circumstances and used Joseph's circumstances for his good.

Lift Your Level Of Expectancy

Stop worrying about what the devil is trying to do and get zeroed in on what God is trying to do.

God can use your problems – the sicknesses in your body, your financial needs, your family problems – because your circumstances, your extremities, are God's opportunities.

When you go through the valley of the shadow of death, God will use that circumstance to prove His faithfulness. He will use it to prove that He will never leave you, nor forsake you (Hebrew 13:5).

Your circumstances are an opportunity for you to draw near to God and for God to reveal Himself to you through those circumstances in a greater way than He ever has before.

The siege of Samaria and the famine the Israelites endured were divine opportunities for God to intervene in their circumstances and to show Himself strong, as Jehovah, and provide for their needs. In other words, He was bringing glory to Himself through the circumstances in their lives.

Step 3–See Your Problems As Miracle Opportunities

What glory can be realized from the needs and circumstances in your life?

See them as God's opportunity to fulfill His Word to you.

Remember the words I shared with you in Chapter Three. When God told me to take my eyes off the bigness of my circumstances. He said, "I will take you step by step by step, not all at once, and each step will be a miracle."

Refuse to accept your situation as it is. Lift your level of expectancy. Whatever your circumstances may be, you can face them without fear, because you know that God wants to use your circumstances on your behalf.

Begin each new day expecting a miracle. Believe He is working on your behalf. Praise Him for it.

Change your way of thinking.

Replace fear with courage, worry with trust, and doubt with a simple loyalty to God and His Word.

God will change your problems into miracles.

Chapter Five

Step 4
Realize That in Every Promise Of God Contains The Seed For Your Miracle

Right now God has a miracle for your needs. The seed – the potential for the fulfillment of that miracle – is in the promises God has made to you in His Word. You do not have to struggle to receive your miracle. God has already spoken the Word to meet your circumstances. The promise is yours. Simply reach out now and take God's promise, His miracle provision for your life.

In the previous four chapters, we have been following the events leading up to a great miracle in the life of Elisha and the children of Israel. Each one of the three steps: 1. See God As He Is; 2. Take Your Eyes Off Your Circumstances; 3. See Your Problems As Miracle Opportunities have been preparing you, getting you into a position where you can experience a miracle in your life.

In our miracle story, we have brought Elisha through some very discouraging circumstances. To the natural eye it was an impossible situation, yet Elisha faced the terrible conditions of the famine, and the king's messenger who came to cut off his head, with a word from God (II Kings 7:1). He faced his circumstances with courage, confidence, and a loyalty to God and His word.

Now let us focus our attention upon the word God gave Elisha to meet the circumstances he was facing. Then Elisha said, *Hear ye the word of the Lord; ... Tomorrow about this time shall a measure of fine flour be sold for a shekel, and two measures of barley for a shekel, in the gate of Samaria.*

How can you make such an unbelievable statement, Elisha? Don't you know that what you're saying is impossible?

These words, coming from God through Elisha, challenged the existing circumstances. They were not based upon presumption, a hoping, Elisha's intuition, or man's ability. The message was not based upon anything Elisha had seen with his natural eyes. The circumstances were still the same. People were still dying.

Elisha spoke forth the word based upon his confidence in a miracle-working God. He knew what he was saying sounded ridiculous to the king and his men, but Elisha also knew that whatever God promised would come to pass. There was no doubt, no hesitation, just a simple loyalty to God.

Just as God's word came forth to meet the needs of the people of Samaria, His Word is full of His promises to you. Regardless of how distressing or how impossible your situation may seem, there is a word from God to meet your need.

Miracles Are Based Upon God's Word

Miracles, from their promise to their fulfillment, are based upon God's Word. And, in order to be able to see the fulfillment of God's promises to you, you must have a clear understanding of the Word of God.

You must realize that every promise of God (the Word) contains the Seed for Your Miracle.

As a child growing up, I was taught to honor and reverence the Old Testament Scriptures. I respected them, but they were only words in a book to me. They had no real affect on my life. But after I accepted Jesus Christ as my personal Savior, the Bible became more than just a book.

As I read, I was no longer reading about people, historical places, and events that happened thousands of years ago. God began to speak to me through its pages. I began to understand that the promises God made in His Word belonged to me! My Bible became my most valuable possession. I literally spent hours and hours at a time devouring its pages.

In later years, when it was necessary for me to leave my wife, Theresa, and my children for months at a time to travel from country to country training Nationals and conducting crusades, the Word of God comforted and strengthened me. It was my source of strength. When I became mentally and physically exhausted from the demanding schedule I kept, in order to take the Gospel to the nations of the world, the Word of God refreshed me and kept me going.

In times of my deepest needs, I have clung to the Word of God, and as a result, I have experienced many miracles. The Bible, the written Word of God, is very precious to me. God has shown me through the experiences I have faced that the Word of God is more than just the written Word of God, the Bible. It is also the Living Word, Jesus Christ, Himself.

One of the reasons why more people do not have miracles in their lives is that they do not understand the Word of God, and they do not realize what is available to them through the promises contained in the written Word of God.

To many people, the Bible is just a history book filled with interesting stories about the Jewish nation and about a good Man named Jesus Who lived over two thousand years ago, Who had power to heal.

Most people will agree it is a good book to live by, but too often they feel it is outdated and does not apply to them and the needs of the world today.

The Bible could easily be considered the best selling book of all time. It has been translated into almost every known language and has been distributed throughout the world. In America, there are copies of the Bible placed by the faithful Gideons in almost every hotel and motel room in the country. In most homes there is at least one Bible, and in some homes as many as eight or ten.

Yet, with this widespread circulation and knowledge of the written Word of God, people are still living defeated lives. They cannot cope with their problems. They are fearful, sick, discouraged and don't know what to do or who to turn to.

These people remind me of the millionaires we often read about in the newspapers who are dressed in rags and live on the streets or in run-down, one-room shanties. They spend their lives rummaging through the garbage cans of the city for their food and clothing, when, in reality, they could be dressed in furs and diamonds, live in mansions, and enjoy gourmet dining every day of their lives.

There are some Christians today who are living in the rags of this world; living day after day below the blessings God has promised them, not necessarily because they choose to do so, nor because they have not heard nor read about God's miracle provisions for them, but simply because they have not received a true revelation of the Word of God and have not made it part of their daily living.

Some people have a difficult time just believing miracles are possible. They do not understand how they can experience a miracle in their own life simply by trusting God to fulfill His promises to them. It sounds too easy.

Others feel they must perform good deeds before they can qualify to receive a miracle in their life. There are also those who struggle to attain the great faith they feel is necessary to believe God for a miracle.

There are still others who, when their back is up against the wall, and someone tells them they can find the answers and solutions to their problems in the Bible, they think it is a cop-out. These people ask the questions: Sure, the Bible is a good Book filled with promises, but does it really work? How is it possible to see those promises become a reality in my life? Can the Word of God be trusted? How can the Word bring a miracle in my life?

The Bible Is God's Voice Speaking To You

How do you relate to the written Word of God? When you see it lying on the coffee table or book shelf, do you see a good book, filled with stories and words of wisdom, or do you recognize it as the voice of God speaking to you?

Actually, that is exactly what the written Word of God is. It is God's voice, one of God's methods of communicating with you. In it God gives you directions on how to establish a personal relationship with Him, how to be happy and successful, how to raise a family, and how to be blessed financially.

In the written Word, God reveals His great love for you and His desire that all your needs be met. Within His written Word He has given you many promises, which I like to call miracle provisions. You see, God's ultimate intention for you as a child of God is total care, total provision.

Through these promises, *miracle provisions*, God has provided for the healing of your body: *But he (Jesus) was wounded for our transgressions, he was bruised for our iniquities: the chastisement of our peace was upon him; and with his stripes we are healed* (Isaiah 53:5).

God has given you *miracle provisions* regarding your finances. He has promised to supply all your needs and to open up the windows of heaven and pour out a blessing upon you (Philippians 4:19, Malachi 3:10).

He has given you *miracle provisions* concerning your family: *Blessed is the man that feareth the LORD, that delighteth greatly in his commandments. His seed shall be mighty upon earth: the generation of the upright shall be blessed. Wealth and riches shall be in his house: and his righteousness endureth for ever* (Psalms 112:1-3).

When you are lonely, fearful, and discouraged, God has a *miracle provision* of comfort, peace, and safety for you. He has promised that He will never leave nor forsake you (Hebrews 13:5). He has promised, *Fear not, for I am with you; Be not dismayed, for I am your God. I will strengthen you, Yes, I will help you, I will uphold you with My righteous right hand* (Isaiah 41:10, NKJ).

The Miracle Book

When you are faced on every side by problems, and there seems to be no way out and no hope in sight, God has a *miracle provision* for you. He promises you that if you have faith ... *ye shall say unto this mountain (your problem), Be thou removed, and be thou cast into the sea; it shall be done. And all things, whatsoever ye shall ask in prayer, believing, ye shall receive* (Matthew 21:21-22).

All of these promises (and many more) belong to every child of God who has accepted Jesus Christ into their life and is walking in obedience to His Word. Within every one of these promises is the power for its own fulfillment.

Once you understand that the same power which created the heavens and the Earth, the sun, the moon, the stars, the flowers and trees, the animals, and every living thing, that same creative power is in every promise God has given to you, you will realize that the Word of God is the most powerful force upon the Earth today. Its power is not limited by any circumstance you may face.

God's Word Possesses The Power For Its Own Fulfillment

The words that came out of Elisha's mouth had the power for their own fulfillment. They were not Elisha's words. They were words from God. Elisha was just an instrument God used to speak forth a word to meet the circumstances the king and the people of Samaria faced.

The fulfillment for the words Elisha spoke forth did not depend upon the king's ability to believe or even upon Elisha's great faith. Oh, yes, it did require faith – a loyalty to God and His Word – for Elisha to speak forth the word, but the word from God possessed enough power within itself to produce the miracle that was needed.

Here was a great need that could not be met by human means, a need that required a miracle, a supernatural intervention from God. God gave Elisha a word to meet that circumstance. Elisha spoke forth the word. The result? A miracle!

It sounds so simple, doesn't it? That's the way God deals with man. He hasn't made it difficult for you to reach Him, neither has He made it difficult for you to receive the miracle you need.

If you have a need that cannot be met by human means, you need a miracle. God has a spoken word to meet that circumstance, and all that He requires of you is that you believe that He is not a liar, that what He has spoken will come to pass.

If it is so easy, why aren't more people receiving miracles?

Man, with all his ideologies and theories, has complicated matters. He has tried to make the promises of God vulnerable to his own ability to produce enough faith to bring them to pass.

When you accept Jesus Christ into your life, you receive a measure of faith as a gift from God (Romans 12:3). You already possess enough faith to receive the miracle you need.

Isn't that a welcome relief! You don't need to wait one minute longer! You don't need to struggle any more! All you simply need to do is to take the word God has spoken, and with a simple loyalty to God, speak forth that word, and your miracle will come to pass.

You see, faith is a simple loyalty to God. You acknowledge that if God has spoken a word, it *will* come to pass.

God wants you to develop your loyalty and trust in Him. When Satan brings circumstances into your life to destroy you, and to accuse God, you can say to that old liar, That's a lie, Satan. I know God. He loves me, and I trust Him completely. Regardless of this problem I face, I know God is going to work all things for my good.

Imagine for a moment what would happen if, while I was ministering in a crusade in another city, someone were to call my wife, Theresa, and say, I saw your husband in a bar the other day. He was with three or four women, and they were dancing and drinking and having a wild party. I just called because I thought you would want to know.

What do you think Theresa would do? Would she drop everything, get on a plane, and fly to the city where I was staying, and confront me with accusations she had heard? No, she wouldn't do that.

She would say to the individual who called her, You've got the wrong man. My husband would never do what you have accused him of. And with that, she would hang up the receiver.

Why?

Because she knows me and is loyal to me, and she knows I am loyal to her.

God wants you to develop such a loyalty to Him that regardless of how bad things look or how long you may have to wait, you will be able to say concerning His promises to you, God said it. I believe it. That settles it for me! This is what faith is really all about, a simple loyalty to God.

It is impossible for God to lie (Numbers 23:19), and His words will never pass away (Matthew 24:35). This is the foundation upon which you can base your loyalty to God. His Word is the only thing in this world that is not subject to change.

Your feelings are subject to change. One day you can be on top of the world and the next day at the bottom of a dark, black hole, trying to find your way out.

Your circumstances are subject to change. Everything may be going smoothly for you one day, and before you know it, the car breaks down requiring major repairs, you lose your job, your best friend turns on you, and the doctors tell you that you have a condition requiring major surgery.

God does not change. He has declared, *For I am the LORD, I change not...* (Malachi 3:6). God and His Word are one. *In the beginning was the Word, and the Word was with God, and the Word was God. All things were made by him; and without him was not any thing made that was made* (John 1:1,3). God and His Word are inseparable, and since God does not change, His Word does not change.

God's Promises Are Not Dependent Upon You

God's Word is absolutely "infallible," which means "there is no margin for error." God has promised that the Word He sent forth into the world would not return unto Him without accomplishing His purpose. *So shall my word be that goeth forth out of my mouth: it shall not return unto me void, but it shall accomplish that which I please, and it shall prosper in the thing whereto I sent it* (Isaiah 55:11).

God is a God of purpose, plan, design, and objectivity. God has a purpose for every word, every promise, He has spoken, and it will accomplish that purpose.

Remember, the power for the fulfillment of God's promises, His *miracle provisions,* is not in you. The seed or power for the fulfillment of God's promises to you is *in the Word.*

Say aloud right now: The power for the fulfillment of my miracle is not in me; it is in God's promise to me.

Receive that revelation into your spirit. Believe it! Act on it! Stop struggling!

God's promises are not dependent upon man's ability to believe. If man does not have faith to believe, that does not affect His promises. They are just as valid: *For what if some did not believe? shall their unbelief make the faith of God without effect? God forbid: yea, let God be true, but every man a liar ...* (Romans 3:3-4).

Do you think for one moment that the king of Samaria had the faith to believe that in a city where people had resorted to cannibalism because of the severe famine that was in the land, that the very next day somehow they would have enough grain to be selling it in the gate of the city?

What about the circumstances in your own life? Perhaps you are confined to bed because of an illness, or maybe your home is being torn apart and there seems to be no hope. Do you think God is depending upon you to bring His promises to pass?

No, my friend, He is not.

Do you know why?

God's Word is just as powerful today as it was the day He spoke the world into existence. The same creative power that enabled Him to say, *Let there be light: and there was light,* that same creative power is still in His Word.

That is why when God's promise is received by a person who is bound by a crippling disease in a wheelchair, there is creative power in that promise to straighten out their limbs and enable them to jump out of that wheelchair completely healed.

That is why when a deaf person receives God's promise into his heart, the creative power of God Almighty is there to create new eardrums if necessary to restore his hearing. That is why when a blind person receives God's *miracle provision* of healing into his heart and demonstrates a simple loyalty to that promise, God can create new eyes or repair damaged retinas or eye muscles.

There is creative power in God's Word!

God sent His Word into the world for a purpose. *And the Word was made flesh, and dwelt among us ...* (John 1:14). The Living Word, Jesus, came to Earth with a purpose to fulfill. Jesus didn't just come to carry your sins and sicknesses and nail them to a cross.

Yes, He came to die. But, everything that man lost as a result of the curse through his disobedience in the Garden of Eden, Jesus came to restore. The Living Word came to restore man to unbroken fellowship and communion with the Father and to set him totally free from all the works of the devil, including sin, sickness, and death.

The Living Word fulfilled His purpose. He defeated Satan once and for all. He ascended back into heaven to the Father. The price is paid. The work is done. Today, He sits at the right hand of the Father making intercession for you (Hebrews 7:25).

The Living Word has made it possible for you to have access to all the promises of God contained in the written Word.

He has promised you ... *that whatsoever ye shall ask of the Father in my name, he may give it you* (John 15:16).

Knowing that God's Word does not change, that there is no margin for error, and that God has promised you that His Word will never fail, you can agree with that Word, and receive it into your spirit, and God will bring His promise to you into effect.

Don't Give Up!

What would you say about the probability of a 100-year-old man and a 90-year-old woman having a child?

Sounds impossible, doesn't it? Well, it is impossible in the natural realm, but with God, *all* things are possible!

God gave Abraham a promise when he was 75 years old. God told Abraham: *And I will make of thee a great nation, and I will bless thee, and make thy name great; and thou shalt be a blessing: And I will bless them that bless thee, and curse him that curseth thee: and in thee shall all families of the earth be blessed* (Genesis 12:2-3). Abraham *received* this promise that He would be the father of a great nation.

Ten long years passed, and the promise was not fulfilled. Abraham was still childless. Abraham had not given up hope, but he was beginning to wonder how God was going to fulfill His promise.

God spoke to Abraham in a vision and reassured him that He had not forgotten His promise to him. God said, ... *Look now toward heaven, and tell the stars, if thou be able to number them: and he said unto him, So shall thy seed be"* (Genesis 15:5). Abraham believed this promise. He had a loyalty to God. If God said it, that settled it!

Abraham's wife, Sarah, was 75 years old at that time. She was tired of waiting for the fulfillment of God's promise, so she decided she would take matters into her own hands. She persuaded Abraham to have a child by her maid, Hagar.

How typical Sarah's actions are with the way some people treat God's promises today. People acknowledge His promises, but when they fail to see results when they want them, they often take matters into their own hands. Their eyes are fixed upon a manifestation instead of the unchanging, infallible promises of God.

Abraham went along with Sarah's scheme, and a year later a son was born to Abraham by Hagar.

Fourteen more years passed, and God, once again, confirmed His promise to Abraham. He revealed to Abraham that Sarah would be the mother of nations. God told him that Sarah would bear him a son, and through this son, this promise would be fulfilled.

No doubt, Abraham had reconciled himself to the fact that since he and Sarah were beyond the age of having children, the fulfillment of God's promise would come through his son, Ishmael.

What was Abraham's initial reaction?

Abraham laughed to himself, and said, How is it going to be possible for a man, who is 100 years old, and a woman, who is 90, to give birth to a child? (Genesis 17:17).

The fulfillment of God's promise was not in man's ability. It was not in Abraham. God's promise (His Word) to Abraham had within it the power for its own fulfillment.

God gave a third confirmation of His promise to Abraham. Angels appeared unto him and delivered a word from God. They told him again that Sarah would bear a son. Sarah overheard the conversation, and she also laughed to herself. How am I possibly going to bear a son? I'm well past the years of childbearing, and Abraham is an old man. It's impossible.

Abraham and Sarah both laughed at this promise, but that did not make God's promise void. God had spoken a word, and it would surely come to pass.

Twenty-five years after Abraham received and believed God's promise, he received the fulfillment of that promise. A miracle took place. Sarah, well past childbearing age, conceived and bare a son, through which God would bless the nations of the world.

In this miracle story, there are two very important truths that will help you in receiving a miracle from God:

1. Don't give up! Don't put any limits upon God. Don't fix your eyes upon an outward manifestation. Fix your eyes on His Word. Trust God to perform a miracle in your life at any time, using any method He chooses. Whether it takes one minute, a day, a month, a year, or many years, don't give up. The power for the fulfillment is in God's literal Word.

2. Don't take matters into your own hands. Whatever God promises, He will do. You don't need to struggle to make it happen. Don't compromise the promise God has given you by mixing your own man-made strategies to "help" God fulfill His promise to you.

Receive God's Promises Into Your Spirit

Before the Word of God can produce a miracle in your life, you must first receive it into your spirit. The natural mind cannot accept the fact that it is possible for a 90-year-old woman to give birth to a baby; that it is possible for a person blind from birth to see; or, that exactly the right amount of money to meet a financial need can come from unexpected sources precisely at the moment it is needed. And, because the natural mind is not capable of understanding miracles, God's Word, His promises to you must bypass your natural mind.

Out of desperation have you ever gone to a friend with a seemingly impossible situation, and they have encouraged you by sharing a particular promise from the written Word of God? And because you were desperate, you decided to see if that promise would work for you? You may have repeated it over and over several times a day, but no matter how hard you tried, nothing happened. You may have thought to yourself, If only I had more faith. I know the Word of God is true, and it has worked for my friend, but why isn't it working for me?

When people reach the place where it seems God's promises, His *miracle provisions* of healing, deliverance, and spiritual and financial prosperity are not being manifested in their lives, it is not because God's Word is powerless; it is not necessarily because they do not have enough faith. It is because the Word has not penetrated into their spirit.

The Word of God (Living and written) is a seed which must be planted deep within your spirit before it will grow and produce the miracle you need.

To illustrate this point, let's first consider the natural laws governing the growth of a seed. For example, imagine you are planning to grow a vegetable garden in your backyard. In that garden you plan to have two or three rows of corn. What would happen if you ignored the instructions regarding the planting of those seeds, and you just threw them on the ground, covered them up with a little dirt, and sprinkled them with a little water?

You would be greatly disappointed when week after week passed and nothing happened, when not even a trace of a sprout came up.

First, a seed of corn contains the ability within itself to produce a corn stalk with ears of corn. But, there are certain natural laws that govern its ability to grow. A very basic first step is that it must first be planted. Even though it has the ability to produce a stalk of corn, it will not produce unless it is planted.

Second, it cannot be planted too shallowly or too deeply into the ground. If it is planted too shallowly, either the birds will eat it, or the wind will blow it away. If it is planted too deeply into the ground, it will not be able to grow because of a lack of oxygen.

Thirdly, before the seed will grow, temperature and moisture conditions must be met. If the soil is too wet or too dry, the seed will not grow.

After all of these conditions are met, something begins to happen. The seed begins to swell. The outer shell breaks, and the seed begins to grow. The roots appear first, and before long the shoot breaks through the ground.

Now, let's compare God's promises to this seed. (Remember, that every promise of God contains the seed, the potential, for its fulfillment.)

Let's imagine that you need a financial miracle. God has already spoken the Word to meet your need. He has given you miracle provisions that promise you that if you will give, it will be given back to you (Luke 6:38). If you will give a tenth of your earnings into God's work, He will pour out a blessing upon you that you will not be able to receive (Malachi 3:10).

These promises, like seeds, must be planted in your spirit. They will not grow if they are planted in your mind. The fact that you have heard these promises with your natural ear is not sufficient. The fact that you have seen these promises manifested in the lives of others is not sufficient. Your spirit must become totally saturated with these promises before you will be able to see the manifestation of your miracle.

Also, before these promises will produce a financial miracle for you, you must be sure that the spiritual laws and conditions presented in those promises are followed. You must be giving a tenth into God's work before you can expect to receive a blessing you will not be able to contain. God will open up the windows of heaven. And, once you begin giving, you will find the more you give, the more God gives back to you.

But this I say, He which soweth sparingly shall reap also sparingly; and he which soweth bountifully shall reap also bountifully. And God is able to make all grace abound toward you; that ye, always having all sufficiency in all things, may abound to every good work. (II Corinthians 9:6,8)

After these conditions are met (God's promise is planted in your spirit, and you are obeying the spiritual law presented in the promise), something will happen. The seed of God's Word will begin to grow within you, and as you begin to speak forth that promise, you will receive your miracle.

How is it possible for an individual to be sure God's promises have penetrated into his spirit?

The best way any person can be sure that God's promises are not lodged somewhere in their natural mind is to be sure that both the Living Word, Jesus Christ, and the written Word have taken up permanent residence within their heart. Jesus said, *If ye abide in me, and my words abide in you, ye shall ask what ye will, and it shall be done unto you* (John 15:7). This is the secret to living a life filled with miracles.

Reading and studying the written Word of God is good. However, in order for it to work for you, you must meditate on it continually throughout the day – at home, at school, on the job, and even while you are relaxing. Allow God's promises to penetrate any doubt or fear that you may have.

It sounds so simple, doesn't it? God has promised you that if you would make the Living and written Word part of your life, that you could ask ANYTHING, and He will do it for you.

Be It Unto Me According To Thy Word

God has not made it a difficult procedure for you to come to Him and have your needs met. He loves you, and He would not have given you so many promises in His Word requiring divine intervention if He did not intend to work miracles on your behalf. All that He expects of you is that you believe and have a simple loyalty to Him that He will do what He has promised.

God has already spoken the Word to meet your need. He is not depending upon you to bring His promises to pass. His Word possesses the power for its own fulfillment. When the promise comes, faith comes with it.

Once God's promise is planted within your spirit, you can enter into a new rest, a place of confidence and security. You may not understand how, when, or why, but you know that God's promise will bring you the miracle you need.

One of the greatest and most significant miracles ever recorded involves a young virgin named Mary. As we look at her reaction to the promise that was given to her, put yourself in her place. How would you have reacted?

Mary was a young Jewish girl who was engaged to be married to a man named Joseph. During the time of her engagement, God sent an angel with a special word, a promise from God: *Fear not, Mary: for thou hast found favour with God. And, behold, thou shalt conceive in thy womb, and bring forth a son, and shalt call his name JESUS. He shall be great, and shall be called the Son of the Highest: and the Lord God shall give unto him the throne of his father David: And he shall reign over the house of Jacob for ever; and of his kingdom there shall be no end* (Luke 1:30-33).

The words the angel spoke to Mary were far beyond her comprehension. Through this angel, God was telling her that she was going to conceive and give birth to the promised Messiah, the Son of God.

Can you imagine the emotions Mary was experiencing at that moment? What joy she must have felt. Out of all the women in the Jewish nation, God had chosen her. It was almost overwhelming. What a sacred responsibility she had been given, to be the mother of the Son of God!

But, at the same time, she was also confused and afraid. She asked the angel, How can this possibly come to pass? I am a virgin. It is impossible for a virgin to conceive.

The angel said, That which is born in you will be born of the Holy Ghost. The Holy Ghost shall come on thee. The power of the Highest shall overshadow thee. That holy thing which shall be born in thee shall be called the Son of God. Mary, you are going to give birth to the Son of God.

He said, *Mary, what seems impossible to man is possible with God* (Luke 1:37).

The angel brought a word from God, and with that spoken word from God came faith.

It did not depend upon a faith that Mary could somehow develop. It did not depend upon a faith that Mary could somehow demonstrate. The faith, the power, was already in the word spoken.

God was not depending on whether Mary could demonstrate the faith for this miracle. God's Word was not vulnerable, depending upon Mary. All God was looking for was a yielded vessel.

Mary did not wonder if she had enough faith to believe the promise. She simply yielded herself to God, and said to the angel, Though I do not understand it, though I cannot comprehend it, be it unto me even as thou hast spoken it (Luke 1:38).

Mary first received the Word, the promise from God, into her spirit before the promise was manifested in her physical body. The faith was present in that promise, and the incorruptible seed of Jesus Christ was created and grew within her womb until the appointed time when she gave birth to the Son of God.

Regarding the miracle you need in your life, God wants you to develop this same trust, this same dependence upon God, that Mary possessed, when you can say, Lord, be it unto me as You have spoken it.

There is no more need for you to wonder if you have faith or if you're going to be able to believe God's promises to you. God knows you, and He deals with you just as you are.

God is a God of miracles. When He sends the Word, He sends the faith and the power for its fulfillment. When that Word takes root within your spirit, the faith and power is released, and the promise is fulfilled in your life.

As in the story of Elisha and the people of Samaria, the miracle was within the power of the Word itself. It was in "Thus saith the Lord." Stand firm on God's Word, His promises, to you, and you will see the Word come to pass right before your eyes.

Whatever your need is, it is not too big for Him! Take the next step toward your miracle. Realize that every promise contains the seed for your miracle. Receive the spoken Word of God, His promises, into your spirit. In total dependence upon Him, say, Be it unto me as You have spoken.

The Miracle Book

Chapter Six

Step 5
Plant A Miracle Seed By
Acting On God's Word

It's time for a miracle! In the previous chapters you have been taking one step at a time toward the miracle you need. Now, it is time for you to take one last and very important step. You must ACT upon the Word, the promise, God has given you regarding your need.

What is the circumstance you are facing that requires a miracle?

Do you have a physical disability? Heart condition? Arthritis? Loss of hearing? Perhaps you have a family member who is confined to a wheelchair or a friend who is suffering from diabetes or cancer. Or, you may be suffering from a chronic sinus infection, severe headaches, ulcers, or a nervous condition, and you have told yourself that you are just going to learn to live with that condition.

My friend, God has already spoken the Word which will heal you, your family, and your friends, and set you free from every disease and every physical limitation. God sent forth the Living Word, Jesus Christ, into the world for a purpose – to destroy sin, sickness, and death! And, remember, God has promised that His Word will not return unto Him without accomplishing that purpose.

Jesus Christ has already paid the price for your healing: *Who his own self bare our sins in his own body on the tree, that we, being dead to sins, should live unto righteousness: by whose stripes ye were healed* (I Peter 2:24).

The work has been done. You *are* healed.

Whoever you are, whatever physical condition you may be in, this is God's promise, His *miracle provision* of healing for you. You don't need to struggle to believe. The faith is present in the Word. The power is in the Word. The Word cannot change. It will accomplish its purpose in your life and in the lives of those you love.

Once you *receive* this promise within your *spirit*, there is only one thing left for you to do: You must act on it.

In your life right now, you may be facing serious financial difficulties. The bank may be threatening to foreclose on your home. In your business, you may be experiencing costly setbacks, or you may be struggling from paycheck to paycheck just to pay the rent and keep food on the table.

God has promised you that He will supply all your needs according to His riches in Christ Jesus (Philippians 4:19).

If you will seek first the Kingdom of God and His righteousness, then the money for your rent, your food, your clothing, and all these other things will be supplied (Matthew 6:31-33).

God has promised that if you will hear and become a doer of His Word, He will cause you to prosper in all that you do (Deuteronomy 29:9).

Have these promises penetrated your spirit? You must not allow your circumstances – the overdue bills, or your lack of money – to hinder you from receiving these promises from God. And, before you can receive the fulfillment of any of these promises, before you can experience a miracle, you must also begin to act on them.

In your family, you may be facing serious problems. Your husband or wife may have filed for a divorce. Your children may have become involved in drugs. Your home may be filled with strife and turmoil. Or, possibly there are strained relationships and there is a need for better communication, more understanding, more love.

Step 5—Plant A Miracle Seed By Acting On God's Word.

God has promised you that if you will believe and have confidence in Him, that what He has promised will come to pass. You will be able to ask anything you desire, and it will be done. *Therefore I say unto you, What things soever ye desire, when ye pray, believe that ye receive them, and ye shall have them* (Mark 11:24).

This promise is yours, and it will work for you and your family once it has grown within your spirit and you have begun to act on it.

Faith Is A Fact, But Faith Is An Act!

In our miracle story concerning the great famine in Samaria, the key ingredient which brought the miracle was not the great faith that Elisha possessed. The key ingredient was the word from God. The manifestation of the miracle was a direct result of the words spoken by Elisha. Just as God had promised, the very next day ... *a measure of fine flour was sold for a shekel, and two measures of barley for a shekel, according to the word of the LORD* (II Kings 7:16).

The words from God that came through Elisha's lips possessed the power for their own fulfillment. However, before these words could produce the manifestation of the miracle, an action was required by Elisha. His loyalty and confidence in God's faithfulness to fulfill His word and perform a miracle was not enough. Elisha was required to act, to speak forth the promises BEFORE he saw any visible manifestation.

Elisha did not know how God was going to perform this miracle, but based upon his past experiences, he knew it was enough to simply speak the word God had given him, and God would do the rest.

God could have opened the "windows" of heaven and rained down food as He had done for the children of Israel while they were wandering in the wilderness for 40 years.

He could have miraculously filled every empty cupboard in every house in the city with food.

On this particular occasion, however, God chose to use the most unlikely candidates – four dying lepers. These men were not allowed inside the city of Samaria, because as lepers, they were considered unclean.

As they sat outside the gate of the city, they began to take a serious look at their condition. If they stayed where they were, outside the city, they would die of starvation. If they entered the city, they would be put to death. The only alternative they could possibly see was to surrender to the Syrians who were camped outside the city. There was a slight chance the Syrians would spare their lives.

They all came to the same conclusion. It was time to act! They said to one another... *Why sit we here until we die?* (II Kings 7:3).

Out of desperation they got up at twilight and headed toward the Syrian camp.

As they were going, a miracle happened. God supernaturally intervened in their circumstances. God will not allow His Word to be vulnerable. He always goes before it. He went before His Word to bring it to pass.

During the early morning hours, God caused the Syrians to hear noises which sounded like chariots, horses, and marching men. Thinking a great army was approaching, fear gripped the Syrian soldiers. They left everything – their tents, horses, and all their belongings – and ran for their lives.

The lepers were the first to see and experience the fulfillment of God's promise to Elisha and the people of Samaria. They went into the Syrian tents and ate and drank until they were filled. Later they went back to the city and told the porter at the gate that the Syrians had fled, leaving everything behind.

The king of Samaria sent messengers to see if the lepers were telling the truth. The messengers returned with a good report, and the people of Samaria gathered up the spoils from the Syrian camp.

God performed a miracle to meet the needs of the people and to confirm His Word.

God does not want you to wait, like these four lepers, until you are at a point of desperation to act upon His promises. He wants you to live a life where miracles are a natural occurrence in your life. Every time you have a need, which cannot be met by human means, He wants you to act, to speak His Word and receive a miracle.

These four lepers more than likely had not heard about the promise given to the people of Samaria through Elisha. They were simply tired of sitting around waiting to die. They marched into the Syrian camp *hoping* their lives would be spared.

As a child of God, you do not have to face your circumstances hoping or presuming. God will meet you at the point of your need. You can face your problems *knowing* God's Word cannot fail.

If you have been facing desperate circumstances day after day, week after week, there is no reason for you to wait one minute longer. The Living Word is within you. You have God's promises, which possess the power for their fulfillment. Decide today that you are going to plant a miracle seed by acting on God's promises to you.

As you take this fifth step to receiving your miracle by *acting on the promises God has given you,* you must forget your preconceived ideas of how, where, and when you want God to work a miracle in your life. You must be willing to forget your pride and what others will think about you. You must rid yourself of any self-sufficiency or dependence upon man's natural abilities and trust completely in God.

There was a man in the Old Testament who desperately needed a miracle of healing in his life (II Kings 5:1). Naaman held a position of honor and prestige. He was a captain of the host of the king of Syria. He was a strong man who had fought and won many battles, but he was a leper.

Imagine, if you can, this Syrian captain putting on his best uniform and setting out for Elisha's house in his chariot. He is excited about the possibility of being healed from his leprosy!

He begins to picture in his mind how he is going to receive his miracle: Surely out of respect for me as a captain in the Syrian Army, Elisha will personally greet me. Then, he will probably call upon his God and will wave his hand over me, and I will be healed.

Can you identify with Naaman? Have there been times in your life when you have needed a miracle from God, but even before you have called upon Him in prayer, you have already decided how, when, and where you want it done?

Naaman was totally unprepared for what happened. Elisha didn't even take time to come out to greet him properly. He sent his messenger. And, instead of offering a prayer, Elisha told him to go wash in the Jordan River seven times, and he would be healed.

How ridiculous! What possible reason could Elisha have for me to wash in the Jordan River? There are beautiful rivers in Damascus where I could have gone to wash. Have I come this far just to be told to go wash in the muddy river?

Naaman was furious. His heart was filled with pride, and he refused to obey the words that Elisha had spoken. He jumped into his chariot and started on his journey home.

His servants caught up with him and tried to reason with him. *Why are you so angry, Naaman? If Elisha had asked you to do some noble deed or give a certain sum of money, wouldn't you have done it? What have you got to lose?* (II Kings 5:13).

Step 5–Plant A Miracle Seed By Acting On God's Word.

Naaman was faced with a decision. He could act on the words God had given Elisha – do things God's way – and receive his miracle, or he could refuse to act, go his own way, and die a leper.

Naaman reconsidered. He forgot about what other people would think. He was desperate. He received the word from Elisha and he acted on it. When he came up out of the water the seventh time, he was healed.

God's promise was received and acted upon before it was manifested. When Naaman acted on God's words, spoken to him through Elisha, it brought the miracle he needed.

In the New Testament, there are many other examples of how God required individuals to act upon the spoken Word before a miracle was manifested. Jesus said to the man with a withered hand,...*Stretch forth thine hand*... (Mark 3:5). He said to the paralyzed man,...*Arise, and take up thy bed, and walk*...(Mark 2:9).

On one occasion when ten lepers approached Jesus for a miracle healing, Jesus told them to go show themselves to the priest. It took an act of faith for these leprous men to turn around without any visible manifestation or sign of healing and go show themselves to the priest. But as they acted on Jesus' words, as they went on their way, they were cleansed and made whole (Luke 17:11-14).

Realign Your Thinking With God's Word

In this book I have shown you step by step how God met Elisha, the people of Samaria, and four lepers at the point of their need with a miracle. Now, it is time to apply these steps and experience a miracle in your circumstances.

In this chapter I want you to focus your attention upon the needs in your life. You have read about the miracles I have shared with you that are recorded in the Bible. In the final chapters of this book you will be reading about five of the many miracles God has performed in my life. That is not enough. Simply reading about the miracles that have happened in the lives of others is not enough to bring you the miracle you need. You must become involved on a very personal level, and that is what I am asking you to do now.

At the end of this book there is a very simple exercise I want you to complete as you apply these five steps to your circumstances.

What is the circumstance in your life that you are facing that cannot be met by human means?

Sickness, financial problems, problems with your children, problems with your husband or wife, problems with a habit that may be destroying your life, whatever the circumstance may be, write it down now under Question 1 on page 161.

What are some of the thoughts you have had regarding this circumstance?

For example, let's suppose the problem that you are facing is a long-term disease, such as arthritis, diabetes, or ulcers. When you get up each morning, do you awake expecting God to heal you of that condition? Or, have you accepted it as something you must learn to live with?

Some thoughts which you might have had are:

Why did this happen to me? I guess it's going to be necessary to take medication the rest of my life. I guess I'm never going to improve. I suppose it's not God's will to heal me.

Write your thoughts down now under question 2 at the back of this book.

In chapter one I explained to you how the leading reason why most people do not receive a miracle is that man is limited by his own personal environment – what he hears, speaks, observes, and by what he is taught.

Step 5–Plant A Miracle Seed By Acting On God's Word.

What has happened too many times is that we have aligned our lives with what we have been taught, by what we have seen, by what we have felt, or by what we have heard.

Many times people's thoughts and actions regarding their sickness are affected by what their doctors have told them. The doctor says, I'm sorry, your condition is critical. There is nothing more that I can do or, I'm sorry, you are going to suffer with this condition the rest of your life. You will not be able to do the things you were once able to do.

People hear the doctor's words. They agree with them. They act on them.

As a result, their condition remains the same. They find themselves adjusting their lives to what the doctors have said. For example, if the doctor has told them they probably won't be able to walk around the block, even if they felt as if they might be able to do it, they probably will not try, because the doctor has planted a seed in their mind that they cannot do it.

Please do not misinterpret what I am saying. I believe in doctors, and I am not suggesting that you disregard their instructions. God has given them their medical knowledge to help you.

The point I want you to remember is that the doctor's words are not the final word regarding your sickness, and you should not allow their or anyone else's word to hinder you from receiving a miracle. Even the words of well-meaning friends can hinder you: Now, you know you shouldn't be doing that. Don't forget what the doctor said.

God's written and Living Word is the final word, the final authority!

This truth not only applies regarding the sicknesses you face but any other problem you are facing.

Many people have been taught that the day of miracles is past, that God doesn't perform miracles today. Some have aligned their thinking with this teaching. As a result, they do not expect miracles to happen in their lives, and they do not receive them.

What happens when your body aches with pain? You align your thinking with how you feel. As a result, many times the way you feel hinders you from believing and expecting God for a miracle. You find it hard to believe God to heal you when the pain is still there.

In my own personal life I have had to face this same problem many times. In chapter seven you will be reading about one experience in my life, when I was only 17, of how I refused to allow the excruciating pain I felt to hinder me from believing the promise God had given me that

He would heal me.

Is God greater than this circumstance in your life?

Are you beginning to see that the God Who created the Earth and everything in it is not limited by any circumstance you face? If you believe God is greater than your need, then under question 3, write, Yes, I believe God is greater than this circumstance.

What is God's promise to you regarding your circumstance?

In chapter Five I explained to you how God's promises are like a seed which has the ability to produce a miracle. God's promises are not vulnerable to your ability to produce enough faith. The faith comes with the promise.

You saw how it is impossible to separate God and His Word and that God's promises are infallible. There is no margin for error.

You saw that God's promises to you, the seed for your miracle, must first be planted in your spirit. It is not enough to hear God's promises or see them being manifested in other people's lives. Your spirit must become totally saturated with these promises before you will be able to see the manifestation of your miracle.

The first step in planting your miracle seed is to receive God's promises into your spirit.

Begin to "feed" on the written Word of God. Find the promises God has made to you concerning the circumstances you are facing right now. Write these promises down under question 4. Don't just read them once or twice. Meditate upon them day and night.

Consider the Word of God to be as necessary to your survival as the food you eat or the air you breathe. Allow the Word to live and grow in you. Jesus said that...*Man shall not live by bread alone, but by every word that proceedeth out of the mouth of God* (Matthew 4:4).

As you begin to "feed" and meditate upon God's Word, you will notice something happening in your life. The Word of God will begin to come forth out of your mouth. Jesus said,...*out of the abundance of the heart the mouth speaketh* (Matthew 12:34). In other words, whatever is planted in your heart will come forth. If negative words, fear, and doubt are in your heart, they will come forth. But if the Living and written Word of God is in your heart, His Word will come forth with the power to bring your miracle.

Have you taken your eyes off your circumstances?

Are you able to see your problems as miracle opportunities?

Write down your answers to the above questions under question 5.

The second step in planting your miracle seed is to realign your thinking with God's Word.

Look at your answers to question 2. *What are some of the thoughts you have had regarding this circumstance?* Are your thoughts in line with God's Word?

If they are not, begin today by conforming them with His promise to you. To illustrate this point, imagine that after many months of unemployment, you get a job, but, you have no means of transportation. You have no money to buy a car, and you have no one to turn to.

What would your thoughts be regarding this problem. Well, there goes my job. I'm not going to be able to work because I don't have a car. I guess I'm a born loser. Nothing ever works out for me.

Once the promises of God are firmly rooted in your spirit, your thoughts will change...I know God has promised to supply all my needs. Somehow I believe He is going to provide transportation for me. I'm not going to worry or be afraid. God knows exactly what I need even before I ask Him.

Not only will your thoughts change, but your level of expectancy will rise. You will find yourself beginning each new day expecting a miracle from God.

You must allow God's Word to control your thoughts. If you have a physical disability, do not allow what the doctors have said, how you feel, or what you see to control your thoughts. Realign your thinking:

God's Word says I am healed. I receive His promise into my spirit and I believe I am going to see the manifestation of that promise in my body. Regardless of how I may feel, I am expecting a miracle from God.

The third step in planting your miracle seed is to act on God's Word by speaking it forth.

There is creative power in God's promises. As God's Word begins to grow in your spirit, and begins to control your thoughts, you are going to be able to boldly speak forth His Word, which will set a miracle in motion.

In our miracle story concerning Elisha and the great famine in Samaria, when do you think the miracle occurred?

Step 5–Plant A Miracle Seed By Acting On God's Word.

Did it happen the moment Elisha spoke the word from God?

Did it happen the moment the lepers decided to march into the Syrian camp?

Or, do you think the miracle took place when the people of Samaria picked up the food, clothing, silver, and gold, and brought it are into the city?

Most people feel that a miracle takes place when they see a physical manifestation, the end result. Actually, a miracle is set in motion the moment the Word is spoken forth.

The miracle for Elisha and the people of Samaria took place when Elisha spoke the words God had given him.

The people of Samaria faced a great need that could not be met by human means, a need that required a supernatural intervention from God. God gave Elisha a word to meet that circumstance. Elisha spoke forth the word. The result: a miracle!

Do not fix your faith upon a physical manifestation. Fix it to the unchangeable, uncompromising Word of God. Do not wait until you see a manifestation or give up if you don't see an immediate change. Believe you have received a miracle when you speak forth the Word.

Remember, you must be willing for God to meet you at the point of your need any time, any place, and through any means He chooses.

God's Word is the final word, over all your circumstances, over all the powerful forces upon Earth, and over any attack from Satan.

When I say that God's Word is the final word, it is not just a saying but a reality, and it is borne out in the very real experience of a dear friend of mine, a Southern Baptist minister.

A graduate of a theological seminary, my friend was taught for 19 years that the days of miracles were past.

He and his lovely wife gave birth to a little baby girl. What should have been a time of great joy was instead a time of great sorrow, because the doctor gave them the sad news that their little baby was born with a muscular defect.

That muscular defect was very similar to cerebral palsy. For five months this minister watched his little baby, Lisa, lie in her crib and never lift her head one inch off the covers.

One day he went into his study and opened his New Testament and began to read. He began to seek God.

For a month he read it over and over and over and over again until the word came alive to this minister. He saw a Christ so filled and so moved with compassion for the needs of the people that his spiritual eyes were opened. He repented of his unbelief and his lethargy, and he was gloriously filled with the baptism of the Holy Spirit.

He began to see Christ as He really is (Step No. 1).

Jesus Christ never "was," and Jesus Christ never "shall be"; Jesus Christ "always" is.

One day my friend determined that the miracle for their little baby is healing – who had been born hopeless and helpless and who was given up by all the doctors of Houston, Texas – was theirs.

He saw his daughter's sickness as an opportunity for God to work a miracle (Step No. 2).

He based that determination upon the promises and the authority of the Word of God.

He took his eyes off the circumstances (Step No. 3).

He told me, "Morris, the miracle of God was in our mouths, and what we had to do was to confess that promise out."

He realized that in every promise of God is the seed for a miracle (Step No. 4).

He and his wife took the promises of God, and every day, many times a day, they began to confess the promises out over their daughter lying on that bed.

He and his wife began to act on God's promise to them. They spoke the Word (Step No. 5).

They said, "With His stripes she is healed" (Isaiah 53:5).

They took the Word...*they shall lay hands on the sick, and they shall recover*...(Mark 16:18), and applied it to their daughter.

They laid hands on her, and they confessed the promise out that "by the laying on of our hands our daughter is healed" (I Timothy 4:14).

They confessed the promise out, "If you ask anything in My Name, I will do it" (John 14:13).

This went on for months.

People from the Baptist church that he pastored came by and said, "How is your daughter?"

They looked at those people, and they said something that most people would criticize them severely for. They said, "She is healed."

I can imagine what some of those people must have thought of their pastor. They must have thought he was going to make a big fool of himself and bring ridicule on their church by saying their daughter was healed when there were no outward manifestations of that healing.

Here this child had been born with this muscular defect and hadn't moved her head one inch in five months, and here was the pastor going around saying, "She's healed. She's healed. She's healed!"

Doctors tell us that if a child is in this condition for seven months, they mark it off as a completely hopeless situation.

The months went by, and the baby's condition remained the same. My Baptist friend didn't give up. He and his wife continued to speak forth God's Word. Just a few days before the seventh month, little Lisa turned over in her crib. Two days later, she sat up all by herself!

The doctors wrote across her case the word "Miracle."

I am not talking about mind over matter.

I believe with all my heart that we must use every positive force that God has placed within our being, and that includes the power of our minds to think positive thoughts, but that is not what I'm talking about.

The miracle that took place for my minister friend was the result of the confession of the promises that he and his wife made. As they confessed the promise out, it brought them the miracle they needed.

I thank God for the many good doctors who are seeking to alleviate the physical suffering of people, and I especially thank God for the good Christian doctors who pray over their patients and seek God's guidance as they minister the healing arts they have learned.

I have nothing against good doctors, but I want you to know that no human power has the final word.

No diagnostician, no pediatrician, no brain specialist, no lung specialist, no cancer specialist, no mere human being has the final word on anything. God has the final word.

Step 5—Plant A Miracle Seed By Acting On God's Word.

My minister friend looked beyond what the doctors had said, beyond what were meant to be kind words of well-meaning but unwise friends, and saw that God's Word was the final word. He took the Word and confessed the promises of God out, and he found the miracle he needed for his child.

Speak Forth God's Word

Remember, there is always a word from God to meet every circumstance in your life!

Say it out loud right now:

There is a word from God to meet every circumstance in my life.

It is time for you to plant a miracle seed. You must:

1. Receive His promise in your spirit;
2. Realign your thinking; and
3. Speak forth the Word.

God is looking for people who have confidence in Him and who are loyal to his Word. He wants you to dare to believe He is not a liar. If He said, "I will heal you," He *will* heal you.

If He said, "I will meet your need," He *will* meet your need.

As you speak forth God's promise to you, realize that it is not your words but God's powerful words that are coming out of your mouth. As you *speak,* believe that you will receive what you have spoken.

Jesus said, *Whosoever shall say unto this mountain (your circumstances), Be thou removed, and be thou cast into the sea; and shall not doubt in his heart, but shall believe that those things which he saith shall come to pass; he shall have whatsoever he saith* (Mark 11:23).

In *every* circumstance you face that seems hopeless, when there seems to be no one who cares, God is there. In every circumstance, there is a *miracle provision* for you...*for (God) hath said, I will never leave (you), nor forsake (you). So that (you) may boldly say, The Lord is my helper, and I will not fear what man shall do unto me (Hebrews 13:5-6).*

Do you realize the full significance of that promise?

God has made this promise to you, and it cannot be changed. The Word has gone forth from His mouth, and it will not return unto Him void, but it will accomplish His purpose (Isaiah 55:11).

Does that mean that maybe one time in your life He will meet you at the point of your need with a miracle?

No! He has promised that He would never leave you in your circumstances. He is with you always. When you face a circumstance in your life *that cannot be met by human means,* then you:

1. See Him as He is;
2. Take your eyes off your circumstances;
3. See your problems as miracle opportunities;
4. Realize that every promise of God contains the seed for your miracle; and
5. Plant a miracle seed by acting on God's Word:

You will begin to live in a rhythm of miracles. Miracles will become a natural part of your life. Plant the Word into your spirit and boldly speak it forth. Because God has promised you:

...I am the LORD that healeth thee (Exodus 15:26).

You can boldly say:

...With His stripes I am healed (Isaiah 53:5).

Because God has promised you:

Give, and it shall be given unto you; good measure, pressed down, and shaken together, and running over, shall men give into your bosom... (Luke 6:38).

You can boldly say:

I will not worry about anything; in everything with prayer and thanksgiving I will make my requests known unto God (Philippians 4:6)

and...

I know that my God shall supply all my needs according to His riches in glory by Christ Jesus (Philippians 4:19).

I will delight myself in the LORD and He will give me the desires of my heart. (Psalms 37:4)

Because God has promised you:

...Blessed is the man that feareth the LORD, that delighteth greatly in his commandments. His seed shall be mighty upon the earth: the generation of the upright shall be blessed. Wealth and riches shall be in his house: and his righteousness endureth for ever (Psalms 112:1-3)

You can boldly say:

Whatever problems arise in my family, I know that everything I ask in Jesus' Name believing, I will receive (Matthew 21:22, John 16:23).

When I need guidance in raising my children, I will acknowledge Him, and He will direct my path (Proverbs 3:6).

Because God has promised you:

There hath no temptation (trial or testing) taken you but such as is common to man: but God is faithful, who will not suffer you to be tempted (tested) above that ye are able; but will with the temptation also make a way to escape, that ye may be able to bear it (I Corinthians 10:13).

You can boldly say:

I will say of the LORD, He is my refuge and my fortress: my God; in him will I trust. Surely he shall deliver me from the snare of the fowler... (Psalms 91:2-3).

and...

Because I have made the LORD, which is my refuge, even the most High, my habitation; there shall no evil befall me, neither shall any plague come near my dwelling (Psalms 91:9-10).

I will both lay me down in peace, and sleep: for thou, LORD, only makest me dwell in safety (Psalms 4:8).

Because God has promised you:

Fear thou not; for I am with thee: be not dismayed; for I am thy God: I will strengthen thee: yea, I will help thee; yea, I will uphold thee with the right hand of my righteousness (Isaiah 41:10).

You can boldly say:

THE LORD is my light and my salvation; whom shall I fear? The LORD is the strength of my life; of whom shall I be afraid? (Psalms 27:1)

and...

The LORD is on my side; I will not fear: What can man do unto me? (Psalms 118:6)

Behold, God is my salvation; I will trust, and not be afraid: for the LORD JEHOVAH is my strength and my song; he also is become my salvation (Isaiah 12:2).

Now, come with me behind the scenes into my personal life and ministry...

At the time of this writing, Dr. and Mrs. Cerullo have been married fifty-five years. Their lives are a living testimony of God's love. Dr. Cerullo has dedicated his life for the past 58 years to reaching the lost and training and equipping Nationals to evangelize their nations and bringing in a harvest of souls worldwide.

God has taken us step by step, miracle after miracle...

(Left) While attending Bible College, my jawbone was broken and the bones in my cheek badly splintered. The doctors said more than likely I would never be able to preach or speak with the normal movement of my jaw, but God performed a miracle (see chapter Seven). (Right) Theresa and I are pictured here shortly after we were married in 1951.

In the mid-1950s, Dr. Cerullo conducted large tent crusades. Giant tractor-trailers carried the huge 120' x 240' tent and equipment from city to city. Large crowds filled the tents night after night with hundreds being saved and healed.

My first overseas crusade was in Athens, Greece, in 1954. During this crusade, Theresa and I learned that it is impossible to outgive God. Read about the miraculous events surrounding this crusade in chapter ten.

Pictured here with me are David (4), Susan (2), and Theresa in 1957, prior to the arrival of our "Miracle Baby," Mark.

I have watched God restore sight to the blind, open deaf ears, and cause the lame to walk...

In the United States, Africa, Mexico, South America and all over the world, I have watched God perform miracle after miracle. During our MTAW Miracle Crusade in Guaquil, Ecuador, December 11, 1998, multiple thousands accepted Christ. Many miracles took place, with wheelchairs and crutches being passed over the heads of the people to the stage.

In Sao Paulo, Brazil, April 9-11, 1998, during the MTAW Crusade, the Pacaembu Stadium was packed to capacity with 25,000 to 30,000 people. Thousands were saved each night, and hundreds were healed from all types of diseases. This boy, paralyzed since birth, stood and walked for the first time!

Chapter Seven

All Right, God, Here We Go!

As I walked briskly toward the steps of the little white church where I was scheduled to preach, my broken jaw held in place by a band tightly wrapped around my head, I realized that in the next few minutes I would either become a laughing stock and disgrace ,or I would experience one of the greatest miracles of my life.

I turned around and took one last glance at my friend as he drove away. I will never forget that moment. With my Bible underneath my arm, and God's promise of healing in my heart, I said, "All right, God, here we go!" I tore off the band holding my broken jaw in place, opened the church door, and walked in.

But before I tell you what God did for me in that little white church in upstate New York, let me share with you the events leading up to this unforgettable experience.

After I left the orphanage at the age of 14 1/2, I went to live with the brother and sister-in-law of the woman who had been instrumental in leading me into an experience of accepting Jesus Christ as my Savior. During the next two years, I began to receive invitations from different churches and various groups to minister.

During this time, I became acquainted with Reverend Nickolas Nikolof, the president of an Assemblies of God Bible college on the east coast, at that time in North Bergen, New Jersey. He was a Russian immigrant with a doctorate degree.

Reverend Nickolas Nikolof became a spiritual father to me. He loved me very much and took a very deep interest in me. He was a very intellectual man. I would go to his house, and we would talk hours for on end.

One day he invited me to be the speaker for one of the chapel services at the Bible college after it moved to a lovely campus in Suffern, in upstate New York. I was scarcely 17 at the time. Out of my love and admiration for him, I accepted the invitation.

After the chapel service he invited me to have lunch with him. I found myself sitting beside a slender young woman with black hair and big brown eyes. We didn't talk much, but when the meal was over, I asked her to go out into the hallway with me because I had something I wanted to say to her.

Now, remember, this was the first time I had ever laid eyes on her, and the first time she had met me. I looked her right in the eyes and said, "I want to tell you something before I leave this Bible college. One day, I'm coming back here, and I just want you to know that I'm going to marry you."

Do you know what she did? She put her hands on the top of her head, screamed, and ran away from me as fast as her legs could carry her.

I went home that day from the Bible school and told the couple I was living with, "Today I saw the young lady I'm going to marry." Of course, they thought I was crazy, but that didn't bother me one bit.

The name of the beautiful young lady I saw that day at the Bible college was Theresa, and a few years later she did indeed become my wife. She was one of the major reasons I decided to go to Bible college.

The following September I registered as a student. I attended classes and studied hard during the week. On weekends I preached at churches and special meetings throughout the surrounding area, and worked various odd jobs to earn a little spending money for socks, toothpaste, etc.

During that first year of Bible college I became the pitcher for the school's softball team. One day while I was pitching, a young man about 6 feet, 2 inches tall hit a line drive like you wouldn't believe. I was standing on the pitcher's mound. I had just turned my head a quarter turn, and the ball hit me smack straight on the side of my head and knocked me out.

Students rushed to me and then took me to the hospital where the doctors examined me. My jawbone was broken in two places, and my cheekbone was very badly splintered. My jaw hung open. I could not close it. Later the doctors told me they believed that I would never be able to preach or speak with a normal movement of my jaw.

The doctor told me he was going to send to New Jersey for a special brace designed to hold my jaw properly in place. He said I would have to wear this brace for at least six months. Until the brace arrived he wrapped an elastic cloth band tightly around my head, which locked my jaw into place.

A few days later I was back in school with this band around my head. I was unable to eat except for what I could get through a plastic straw.

Can you imagine how I felt? Here I was trying to court Theresa, who was engaged to someone else at that time (who, by the way, turned out to be my roommate). I was determined to win her heart. I felt so awkward and self-conscious. I'll never forget how hard it was for me to talk to her with my jaw so tightly bound together.

I had made a commitment to preach in upstate New York in a little Pentecostal church. But now, under these circumstances, everyone expected me to cancel the invitation. I had every intention of canceling. In fact, I did. But one day, during prayer in my room at school, God spoke to my heart. He told me that if I would keep the invitation, He would heal me. I told my friends and fellow students that I was going to keep the speaking engagement and that God was going to heal me.

(Sometimes it's not good to reveal everything that God tells you, unless you are prepared to go through an awful period of criticism and unbelief until it comes to pass.)

The week prior to the meeting everyone was on pins and needles wondering whether this crazy young man named Morris was going to bring a terrible disgrace on the school.

I was expecting to have a small crowd of 10 to 15, but when it was time for the service to begin, the place was packed with about 100 people. It seemed as if the entire student body was there. Because of the limited amount of room, students were standing on the outside, cramming their heads through the doors.

In obedience to the word God gave me, "Go. Be faithful and preach. I will heal you", I walked up the steps of the church and tore off the binding holding my jaw in place. My jaw dropped. The pain was so excruciating it seemed it would be enough to cause four or five people to pass out, but I refused to keep my eyes on my circumstances.

With my jaw hanging down I entered the church, walked down the aisle, and took my seat on the platform. There I sat. I couldn't speak, I couldn't sing, nothing.

The man leading the congregation in worship kept looking over his shoulder at me. He didn't know what to do.

He made the announcements, my jaw was the same. He took up the offering, no improvement in my condition. He led the congregation in song after song, but still no physical evidence of a healing. My jaw was the same. Finally, he mustered up enough courage to introduce me.

With every eye upon me, anxiously waiting to see what was going to transpire, I stepped up to the platform. And the moment I opened my mouth to read the Bible, a miracle took place in front of that congregation.

My jaw miraculously snapped back into place! The bones were instantly healed, and I preached my entire message that night without a problem.

It was not a healing...*It was an instantaneous miracle of God.*

I never wore the special metal brace the doctors ordered. I never wore the binding again.

As a result of that miracle, the Spirit of God came upon that place and started a mighty revival among the students.

In that little white church in New York, a young 17-year-old boy named Morris saw God as He is.

I had been taught at the orphanage about a God Who had worked miracles thousands of years ago. But after this experience ,where God miraculously and instantaneously met me at the point of my need with a miracle, the God of the Old Testament became more than a Being far away in the sky Who had performed miracles in the past. I personally experienced His miracle-working power, and at that moment, I saw Him as a miracle-working God of the present.

I saw a loving Father Who was anxiously waiting to meet me at the point of my need.

I saw a God Who is unlimited and all powerful.

I saw beyond the natural limitations of my broken jaw, and I experienced a supernatural manifestation of God's power and glory.

And so can you!

The Miracle Book

Chapter Eight

After Three Days Of Unconsciousness, God Intervened

Throughout my life I have seen and experienced many miracles. God has placed me in a position where I have had the privilege of praying with many people, and I have seen God's miracle power at work. There are people who might look at me and say, It's easy for him to believe God for miracles. He's a well-known evangelist.

I can understand how easy it would be for an individual to feel this way. Yet, what most people do not realize is that God has brought me step by step to where I am today. There were circumstances Theresa and I faced together as two young, inexperienced kids which were difficult, and our faith was tested.

As I look back over some of those experiences, I can see one very simple, yet powerful, ingredient in our lives that seemed to unlock God's miracle provisions for us.

Theresa and I possessed a simple faith and trust in God and His Word. We were totally dependent upon Him for direction, for food, for clothing, for healing, for finances, for everything. I feel one of the reasons more people do not experience miracles is due to a sense of self-sufficiency they have developed. Some people, when a crisis comes, immediately try to work things out for themselves. Only after they have made a total mess of things, and all their efforts have failed, do they decide to give God a try.

After that unforgettable experience, where God instantly healed my jaw, I continued my studies at Bible school for another year. At the end of my third year, Theresa and I were married, and God called us to pastor a small church in Claremont, New Hampshire.

When we got married, I had $35 in my pocket. We didn't have a bed. In fact, we didn't have any furniture. We slept on the floor for months. We didn't have a car. We borrowed my father-in-law's car for our honeymoon.

We didn't have money for a honeymoon, so we accepted an invitation from some good friends of ours, (who had been in our wedding party) to spend two or three days with them in North Bergen, New Jersey.

After the wedding, we drove to North Bergen. Since our finances were very limited, I decided to take Theresa to a baseball game. It was about all we could afford. When we returned that night to our friends' house, I parked Theresa's father's car, but I forgot to put the brake on or to put the car in gear. We parked on top of a hill.

We got out of the car, but before we were able to cross the street, we heard a loud crash. We turned around to see what had happened. When I saw my father-in-law's car at the bottom of the hill, where it had jumped the curb and smashed into a tree, my heart fell to the pit of my stomach. What would my father-in-law think?

After he had been so generous in allowing us to borrow his car, I couldn't return it to him in that condition.

There was only one thing we could do. At our wedding, we had received $350 cash as gifts from our friends and Theresa's relatives to help us get started in our new life together. The next day, I took that wedding money and spent the day at the repair shop getting the car repaired.

Once again, we were flat broke. All we had was enough money for gas to go back to New Jersey and to get to Claremont, New Hampshire, where we were to begin pastoring.

I will never forget our first meal together in the little three-room apartment we had rented in Claremont. When we arrived, we stopped at a grocery store and bought a couple of cans of food and went to our empty apartment. We had no furniture, no dining room table, no chairs.

After Three Days Of Unconsciousness, God Intervened

We opened a can of Franco-American spaghetti, took out a couple of forks, smiled at each other, and sat down on the floor to eat our first meal together.

We didn't feel sorry for ourselves. We didn't mind going to bed hungry or sleeping on the floor because we were determined to do the Will of God, and we knew He would take care of us. There were times we wondered how God would supply our needs, but we never doubted that somehow, some way, He would supernaturally intervene and meet us at the point of our need.

God taught us to keep our eyes off our circumstances and upon His ability. We did not depend upon our own abilities. We didn't try to work things out our way or depend on others. There were times no one knew the intense struggles we were going through because we were totally depending upon God to see us through.

God blessed our ministry at that small church in New Hampshire. In eight months it grew from a handful of members to the sixth largest Spirit-filled, Charismatic church in all of the six New England states.

Just when we were beginning to enjoy a sense of security, God revealed to me that my work in Claremont was finished and that it was time to go back into full-time evangelistic work.

In my heart I knew God had called me to take the Word of God to the four corners of the Earth. I could not forget the vision God had given me as a young boy of 15. I could not forget the screams and cries I heard of those who had rejected Christ and were confined to the torments of hell.

I didn't have any meetings lined up, and now God was asking Theresa and me to launch out again into the unknown.

I knew what I was supposed do. It was going to be necessary to tell Theresa, who was seven months pregnant, that she would have to give up the security she had and go back to living out of a suitcase, with no home and no security for her or our new baby.

It was not easy for Theresa, but she had already made a commitment to God that she could not break. She had already given herself unreservedly to Him. She had promised God that she would not count the cost – that whatever He wanted her to do, she would obey.

We stepped out in faith, resigned the church, packed up our belongings, and went to Theresa's mother's in Newburgh, New York. From her house we began to fulfill the worldwide call God had placed upon our hearts.

A month or two later, our first baby, David, was born. How proud I was of the son God had given us!

When David was only ten days old, we bundled him up, packed our suitcases, placed them in our car, and headed toward the city, where we would be conducting our next meeting. And, for the next six years of our lives, we traveled as a family across the United States in one crusade after another.

Those were difficult days for us. There were times when we barely had enough money to get from one meeting to the next. I remember on one occasion stopping at a truckstop for gas and going into a restaurant and ordering one bowl of soup, which we shared between us. To help fill our empty stomachs, we ate a lot of crackers. I think we ate more crackers than soup!

Most of the time we stayed in the home of the pastor sponsoring the meeting. The times we could afford a motel room were few and far between. When we did have the opportunity to rent a motel room, we were all crowded into one little room. Theresa stayed busy caring for the children. In the afternoons, Theresa would either schedule the children so they would be asleep, or take them out to feed them so that I could wait upon God and prepare for the evening service.

After Three Days Of Unconsciousness, God Intervened

Between meetings we would return to Theresa's mother's house for a few days' rest. There were times we didn't know where the money was going to come from to pay for the gas to travel to the next crusade, but we knew somehow God would provide.

Many times God would provide for us through church offerings or through gifts from individuals in the church. God also used Theresa's precious grandmother to help us get from one crusade to the next. Almost every time we would go home, she would whisper in Theresa's ear, "You don't have any money, do you?" Theresa would just look at her and smile. And her grandmother would reach down in her pocket and give us five or ten dollars to help us get to our next meeting.

Theresa and I learned at an early age in our lives that we could trust God in every circumstance we faced.

When David was four months old, we faced a situation which, on the surface, seemed hopeless. Theresa had a severe gall bladder attack and lay near the point of death. We had seen God perform miracle after miracle in our crusades, and we were determined to trust Him now during this great crisis in our lives.

Anyone who has seen their loved one suffering intense pain knows that in the natural it is not easy to believe God for a miracle. You must turn your back on unbelief. Satan was trying to use our circumstances to take Theresa's life and destroy our ministry. And although this experience was very painful for us both, God not only met us at the point of our need with a miracle, but He caused our faith to grow even stronger.

We were in Wisconsin holding a crusade. This particular meeting had made newspaper headlines all over the state because John C. Chappel, an avowed Communist and atheist, was won to Jesus Christ.

John Chappel was the owner of the local newspaper. When he saw my ad in the newspaper that said I was going to preach, he got mad. In fact, he got so mad that he came into the meeting with clenched fists. He thought I was a con artist or a crook.

During one of the meetings, the Spirit of God began to speak to him, and in front of about six hundred people, he stood up and ran screaming down the aisle, "Lord Jesus, have mercy on my soul!"

During this crusade we were staying in a rented room in a tourist home, about a block away from the minister's home, who was sponsoring the meeting. In my mind, I can still see the little narrow staircase leading to the little room where we were staying.

One day, while I was preaching at a ministers' fellowship, Theresa became violently ill. She was in so much pain she could not hold David. She knew she needed help, so she put David on the floor, closed the door, and went for help. She half crawled, half walked to the minister's house a block away. The minister's wife called the doctor and then went back to our room to get our baby.

The doctor said it sounded as if Theresa was having a gall bladder attack, and they should get her to the hospital. She was throwing up green bile and was doubled up in terrible pain. This was the third attack she had had, and the pain would not subside.

The minister's wife asked her what to do, and Theresa, with her eyes on a miracle-working God, said very calmly, "Just pray. The Lord knows that I am having a problem, and He will take care of me. We will just wait for Morris."

When I got home from the meeting late that night, I prayed for Theresa and took her back to our room. The circumstances we faced were discouraging. There seemed to be no apparent change in her condition. There was no way out, humanly speaking.

I would take care of David during the day, put him to sleep, and go minister to the needs of others at night without telling my problems to anyone but the Lord.

It was very difficult for me to climb the steps to that little room night after night to find Theresa doubled up in pain. I wanted to take her to the doctors, but with her great faith in God, she would say to me, "No, darling, I'm believing God. God is going to heal me. I am not going to the hospital. I'm not going to be operated on. God is going to take care of me."

That meeting closed, and we were scheduled for another crusade in Wisconsin. I packed up our clothes, picked Theresa up (who was still groaning in pain), carried her down the steps, placed her in the back seat of the car, and we were off again for another crusade.

If I had allowed myself to keep my eyes on the circumstances, and on Theresa's intense pain and suffering, we would not have experienced the miracle we needed.

For weeks Theresa's condition remained the same. I was conducting another meeting where God was performing miracle after miracle. I will never forget how helpless I felt concerning Theresa's condition. One night I laid my hands on a young girl who was totally blind, and God healed her. Yet, that night I had to go home to the motel where we were staying and watch my wife dying. For some reason, I couldn't get a breakthrough for her healing.

For three days and nights Theresa lay almost unconscious. I would continue as before, taking care of David during the day and ministering at night. My heart was deeply burdened for Theresa, but I did not lose my faith and confidence in God.

One day, between meetings, while I was praying, God spoke to my heart. He told me to fast and pray for three days, and on the third day, He would heal Theresa.

We don't always understand the ways of God. And I didn't fully understand why God required me to do this. I had been faithful in ministering to others, and I had spent many hours in prayer for Theresa's healing. (It is important for us to always remember that there is a divine providence of God Almighty that goes beyond our theology.)

In the divine providence of God, He had a plan. I told Theresa that God was going to heal her in three days. I obeyed. I fasted and prayed. On the third night, after praying and fasting, we went to sleep.

The next morning, I felt for Theresa in the bed next to me. She was not there!

I was so startled, I jumped out of bed, and I ran into the bathroom where she was. I said, "Honey, what are you doing up?" She said to me, "Well, darling, didn't you tell me that God said if you fasted and prayed three days that He would heal me? Well, the three days are up. I am healed!"

Through this experience I learned to keep believing God. It was a difficult experience, but God built my faith.

From that day until today, over 51 years later, Theresa has not had a trace of that illness again.

Regardless of the circumstances you are facing right now, regardless of how long you may have waited for your miracle, don't give up!

Keep your eyes upon God. Remember that God can take your circumstances and use them for good. God will always cause you to be victorious when your trust is in Him.

Chapter Nine

Mark, Our Miracle Baby

As a husband, father of three children, and grandfather of seven, I can say that I have learned that God can be trusted with the lives of those dearest to you. Theresa and I have experienced many miracles involving our children. I will be sharing only one with you, which involves our third child, Mark, who we call "our miracle baby."

I am sure there are many more experiences Theresa could share with you about how God supernaturally strengthened and provided for her and the children while I was away for months at a time conducting crusades around the world. But, I have chosen to share this miracle story because I want you to know that regardless of the situation you may face in your family – whether it be a serious illness, a runaway boy or girl, or a companion who is fighting a battle with drugs or alcohol – God cares about you and your family. He will meet you at the point of your need with a miracle.

Excluding my relationship and commitment to God, my family is my most precious possession. Being raised in an orphanage, without any real sense of belonging or being needed, I had promised myself that when my children were born, they would never be without a father.

My mother died when I was just a baby. I do not even have any childhood memories of her holding me in her arms or telling me that she loved me. I have never experienced the loving care and companionship of a father.

When I was placed in the orphanage, my three sisters, my brother, and I were separated, and we grew up as strangers. Because of this lack of family relationships as a child, I looked forward to the day when I would have a family of my own.

During the vision I experienced at the age of 15, when God took me up into the heavens, I surrendered everything to Him, including the very thing that I would hold dearest and closest to me. I gave God my family even before I had it.

I am sure there are many people who may wonder how it was possible for me to leave Theresa alone for weeks and months at a time to raise our children. Had I not surrendered them to God, and committed them into His care, I honestly don't think I would have been able to do so year after year.

It was not easy for me to leave Theresa and the children. Before I would leave for a crusade, I would go into the children's rooms while they were asleep, lay hands on them, and pray for each of them individually. Years later, Theresa shared with me how while I was away, she would find Mark and David in my closet, hugging my clothes, with tears streaming down their cheeks.

The saying that "behind every successful man is a good woman" is so true. Although Theresa was not with me during the crusades while the children were growing up, had she not been willing to stay at home and care for the children, I would not have been able to go.

In all the years that I left Theresa to conduct a crusade in another part of the world, not one time did she complain or ask me not to go. She has faithfully supported me with her love and prayers throughout the years and has always made an effort to meet me at the airport when I returned home.

I have not regretted my decision to commit my family into God's hands because, as I look back over the years, I can see how God has protected and provided for them while I was away fulfilling God's calling on my life.

One incident, which clearly stands out in my mind, where God supernaturally protected Theresa and the children, happened one Thanksgiving while I was away from home. During the night Theresa saw someone walk past her bedroom door, but thinking it was the girl whom she had hired to help around the house, she went back to sleep.

In the morning Theresa was awakened by the doorbell. A man from her church, who helped her take care of our swimming pool while I was gone, was at the door. He showed her how the lock was off our door, and the door handle was broken.

Later the police arrived and walked with Theresa through the house, checking to see if anything was missing. He told her that during the night eight of the neighbors' houses were broken into, and jewelry, furniture, and clothing were stolen. Out of the eight houses, our house was the only one where nothing had been taken. God had miraculously protected her and the children.

You can imagine how I felt leaving her alone again after this happened. Even though I believed God would continue to watch over them, it was hard for me to leave. But, based upon the experiences God had already brought our family through, I knew God could be trusted.

The miracle involving our youngest son, Mark, happened when I was only 26.

Theresa and I and our two children, David, who was about four years old at the time, and Susan, who was about two, were staying in a motel in Plain view, Texas, where we were holding a crusade.

It was on a Sunday afternoon, and I was preparing for the last night of the meeting. Suddenly, I heard Theresa scream for help. I ran outside where Theresa had gone to hang out some diapers on the clothesline outside our motel room. (There were no laundromats in those days.)

I found Theresa doubled up in pain, and she was hemorrhaging. I carried her to our room and called a doctor. The doctor rushed to the motel. He told us that Theresa was probably having a miscarriage and that it was extremely dangerous for her to continue in this condition without going to the hospital.

I took her to the small hospital that was directly across the street from the motel. After examining Theresa, the doctor told me that he felt they should scrape her womb, since in all probability she had already lost the baby. He told me that if there was any life left, there would be extreme malformation of body or mind or both. Suddenly I faced the possibility of losing my dearest possession. Not only was our unborn baby's life at stake, Theresa's life was also in danger.

The doctors offered us no hope. In the natural, Theresa and I faced an impossible situation. We had a choice to make, to listen to the doctors and give up hope, or to believe God for a miracle. I went to Theresa's bedside, and we talked it over. It was a difficult decision for us both. And had I not previously committed my family into God's care, I might have hesitated. But we had both learned to depend totally upon God as our Source. We knew that He was a miracle-working God because we had seen Him perform miracle after miracle.

Theresa looked at me and said, "Morris, if we are having another baby, then the Lord is going to either take care of this baby or take the baby. I am not letting the doctor touch me."

I informed the doctor of our decision. He thought we were foolish, but he said, "All right, but I must tell you the facts. You may not get down the road very far before your wife starts hemorrhaging again. It is possible that she might bleed to death before you could get her to a hospital. Those are your alternatives."

Theresa just looked at the doctor and said, "Well, I am willing to see if the Lord can't take care of me."

When the doctor saw how determined we were in trusting God, he gave Theresa a pillow and a blanket, and with tears in his eyes, he wished us well as we drove off to our next meeting.

We traveled slowly. When we got as far as Memphis, Tennessee, Theresa didn't feel like she could go any further. I got her and the children a room in a motel.

I had a crusade scheduled, and I had to leave immediately in order to get there on time. I left my associate minister with Theresa to take care of her and the children until her mother could get there.

During this experience, I learned not to keep my eyes on my circumstances. I didn't want to leave my wife, who was in critical condition, with two small children in a strange city. But, at the same time, I knew that God wanted me to go and minister to the needs of others and to trust Him to heal Theresa and our unborn baby.

I called Theresa's mother in New York, and she took a train to Memphis where Theresa was. When her mother arrived, they took her to another doctor. He examined her and confirmed what the doctor in Texas had told us. He told her that there was no possible way that she could carry the baby to full maturity. Rather than taking the chance of further complications, he advised Theresa to go into the hospital.

Theresa would not hear of it. She continued to believe God for her healing and for our unborn baby. After a few weeks stay in Memphis, she was able to fly home with her mother, where she stayed for several months until it was time for her to give birth to our baby.

When she was five and one-half months pregnant, she still had felt no sign of life, and when the doctor examined her, he was not able to find a heartbeat. He told her she was being a very foolish girl.

Theresa and I continued to refuse to listen to the negative reports we received. We simply believed that the baby was alive and that the Lord would take care of the situation. All during this time I continued to conduct the meetings I had scheduled while Theresa stayed with her mother.

At the close of one of my crusades, I called Theresa and asked her if she felt like picking me up at the New York airport which was about a sixty-mile drive from her mother's home. I told her we would spend the night in New York so that the trip would not be too difficult for her.

She was seven months pregnant and had been feeling fine, so she packed a few things and came to the airport, to meet me. From the airport, we drove to a hotel in New York City. Just as we were putting the key in the door to our room, Theresa screamed in pain as she once again began to hemorrhage.

I looked at Theresa, doubled up in pain, and I said, "What shall I do? Shall I call the hospital?" Even at that moment I could feel God strengthening us. Theresa looked at me and said, "No, take me home."

The bellman at the hotel helped me get Theresa in the car. Theresa laid down on the back seat. As we got to the outskirts of the city, God directed me to stop the car. I leaned back over the seat, placed my hand on Theresa's stomach, and prayed a very simple prayer.

Theresa fell asleep and didn't awake until the car stopped in front of her mother's house. When she awoke, there was no pain, and no sign of hemorrhaging. God had once again heard our prayers!

On New Year's Eve, while we were at the grocery store, she looked at me and said calmly, "Honey, you had better not get that item because, I'll be going to the hospital tonight and you won't have anyone to fix it for you.

I really didn't know what to think. According to the doctor's timetable, the baby wasn't due. How could she possibly know tonight was the night? I said to her, "You will?"

And just as she said, she went into the hospital that night and on New Year's Day, at 3 a.m., we received our very special miracle from God.

The baby the doctors had told us couldn't survive was born. He weighed seven pounds and one ounce and was perfectly normal!

Through this experience, God taught Theresa and me that even in our darkest moments, He was there with us. He knows how much we are able to bear, and He always answers our prayers on time.

God is concerned about your family needs. If there is a situation in your family that cannot be met by human means – a terminal illness, division and strife, bitterness, problems with rebellious teenagers, problems with a husband or wife who is unfaithful – then you need a miracle. Whatever your problem may be, don t give up.

Apply the five steps I have shared with you in this book. God has a miracle waiting for you!

The Miracle Book

Chapter Ten

The Day God Rained 'Manna' From Heaven To Meet Our Needs

From the very first day I said "yes" to God and surrendered my life to Him at the age of 15, until today, 59 years later, I can honestly say that not one time has God ever failed to provide for my financial needs. There were circumstances that Theresa and I faced together that tested our faith, but through those experiences, God strengthened and increased our faith.

We know what it is like to wonder where the money is coming from to buy food and milk for our babies, to pinch pennies to have enough gas to go from one meeting to the next, and to scrape up enough money to pay our bills.

But, we have also learned that as long as we look beyond our own needs, putting God first in our lives and totally depending upon Him, He will supply our needs, even if He has to open up the "windows" of heaven to do it. Time and time again God has fulfilled His promises to us in the Word: *But seek ye first the kingdom of God, and his righteousness; and all these things shall be added unto you* (Matthew 6:33). *And everyone that hath forsaken houses, or brethren, or sisters, or father, or mother, or wife, or children, or lands, for my name's sake, shall receive an hundredfold...*(Matthew 19:29). *Give, and it shall be given unto you; good measure, pressed down, and shaken together, and running over, shall men give into your bosom...*(Luke 6:38).

I could literally sit by the hours and relate to you miracle after miracle God has given us in establishing the World Evangelism headquarters in San Diego. There were times we faced tremendous challenges, which in the natural seemed impossible, times when just the amount that was needed came precisely at the moment we needed it. Those experiences alone could fill a book.

But the miracle I would like to share with you is a personal one involving God's loving care and provision for a young couple who had always been willing to give everything they had into the work of God.

From the very beginning of our ministry together our first objective has been to minister to the needs of people first. We have never resented one sacrifice we have ever made. We have done it willingly simply because we loved God and because we felt it was His Will.

Almost everything we have ever made has gone back into God's work. As long as I have a roof over my head, food to eat, and my family is provided for, I am perfectly happy. Material possessions have never been very important to me, except when they could be used to build the Kingdom of God.

Theresa and the children continued to travel with me from crusade to crusade until the children were ready to start school. During this time we had managed to scrape up enough money for a down payment on a little house in Newburgh, New York. It was a very inexpensive house, selling for $11,500, which was very reasonable at that time.

It was our first house, our dream house. We were so excited. We watched it being built from the foundation on up to the roof, making sure everything was just right.

We placed a small deposit of $600 to hold the house for us until the escrow closed. The remaining money we put in the bank until the house was finished.

While we were waiting for the house to be completed, we were in Pennsylvania conducting meetings, and God impressed upon my heart that He wanted me to prepare to go to Athens, Greece. I will never forget that experience. I was so excited!

I ran to Theresa and said, "Honey, I think this is it." She said, "What do you mean?" I said, "You know the vision I told you about when I was

15, after I left the orphanage? I think that vision is beginning to take place. I feel God wants me to go to a country called Greece."

I was 23 at the time and still "wet behind the ears." I didn't even know where Greece was!

Two weeks later, after God had revealed to me that He wanted me to go to Greece, guess who I got a letter from? It was from Reverend Koustis, who was Superintendent of the Church of God in Greece. In his letter he informed me that he had been praying, and God had directed him to ask me to come to Greece to conduct a meeting.

I didn't hesitate. I wrote to him immediately and informed him that I would come. I told him that God had spoken to me even before he had written, telling me to prepare to go to Greece.

Theresa and I excitedly began to make preparations for my trip. This was going to be my very first overseas crusade! We decided that after I finished the crusade in Greece that I would fly to Israel, spend a few days there, and then return home. And, after I returned home, we would move into our new house.

We went to the travel agency, and when they told me that a round-trip ticket from New York to Tel Aviv, with a stop-over in Athens, Greece, would be $865.50, my heart sank. The ticket agent might as well have asked for $8,650,000!

Where could we get that much money?

Believing that somehow God would meet this need, we continued with our crusades. I didn't give up! I kept making plans, and we set August as the date for the crusade.

One night, during a series of tent meetings in Pennsylvania, I felt a strong awareness of God's Presence and power which seemed to permeate the place. Outside the tent there were two or three times as many people as we had under the tent, standing outside watching. People by the dozens were coming forward to accept Jesus Christ as their Savior.

God directed me to walk down off the platform to pray for a little farmer woman, whose back was so twisted she was unable to walk erect. As I took her by the hand, God instantly healed her. Her back straightened out, and all the arthritis left her bones. Miraculous healings such as this continued night after night.

About a week later, this same little lady came walking down the aisle and walked right up to the platform and motioned for me to come to her.

I was a little embarrassed, but I walked over to the edge of the platform. She shoved something into my hand. I hurriedly took it, stuck it in my Bible, and returned to my seat.

As the lady was walking away, she looked back over her shoulder to see what I was doing. She turned around, came back up to the edge of the platform, pointed her bony little finger at me, and ordered me to read what she had given me.

I took the envelope out of my Bible, opened it up, and read a beautiful letter in which she expressed her deepest gratitude to God for the healing she had received and to me as His servant. The letter ended by saying, "In memorial to my Lord for the healing of my body, I enclose this gift. I sold my farm a little while before you arrived, and this is some of the money I received from the sale. I want you to have it for your ministry." Tucked inside that letter was a check in the amount of $865.50 – exactly the amount I needed for my trip to Athens!

About a month later, I arrived in Greece and I was so excited. I didn't need any rest. I was ready to preach that night!

Reverend Koustis met me at the airport. He looked so tired and dejected. I thought to myself, Why couldn't he be a little more enthusiastic about me being here?

The Day God Rained 'Manna' From Heaven To Meet Our Needs

On our way into town, I was anxious to know about all the preparations that had been made for the meeting. I said, "How's everything going? Do you have a copy of the handbill that you printed for the meeting? I would like to see it."

He hesitated for a moment, and then he said, "We have a little problem there." I said, "A problem?" He said, "Uh-huh."

I was beginning to sense something was wrong. I tried another question, "When will I be able to meet the committee and all the other preachers and missionaries who are going to be cooperating in the meeting?" Again he said, "We have a little problem there." I said, "A problem?" He said, "Uh-huh. I didn't tell anybody you were coming."

Almost afraid to ask, I said, "Where are we holding the meeting? What's the name of the auditorium?" He said, "We have a little problem there." Well, by this time I was more than concerned. I was a little perplexed. I asked, "What's the problem?" "We haven't rented one yet," he said.

Talk about discouraging circumstances! I had left my wife and children and had traveled over four thousand miles to conduct a crusade, and nothing had been done. No one knew I was coming, no handbills, no advertisements, no auditorium, nothing!

By way of explanation, Reverend Koustis explained that in Greece the only church allowed to function was the Greek Orthodox Church and that it was against the law to print or distribute any literature, print an ad in the paper, to rent an auditorium for a meeting, or to witness. All of these things at that time were punishable by years of imprisonment.

He said, "I bear on my body the marks for preaching the Gospel in this country. I've been in prison. I've been thrown off the mainland onto islands and put in dungeons for weeks and months at a time because I violated the law."

I looked at him and said, "Sir, if you knew all of this, why did you let me come?"

He replied, "When I wrote you and asked you to come, you wrote me back and told me that God told you to come to Greece. I didn't want to say anything to you that would keep you away."

He took me to a little, dark, dingy room in the city where he had arranged for me to stay. It was at the top of several flights of stairs. It had one chair and a bed. There were no sheets and no pillow cases, just an old, smelly, dirty mattress.

I wrote down the man's address, and telephone number where he could be reached and told him to wait until I got in touch with him.

That night was a night to remember. I was in a strange country. I didn't know a soul. I had no one to talk to. I stayed up all night praying.

Early the next morning, I left that awful room. With the little money that I had saved for the trip, I walked the unfamiliar streets of Athens, Greece, with my two suitcases in my hands, to find a place to stay. After I located a room in a little hotel on Constitution Square, I let Reverend Koustis know where I could be contacted should anything develop concerning a meeting.

I locked the door and fell on my face before God. "Oh, Lord, what am I going to do?" No one could help me. I needed a supernatural intervention in my circumstances. I needed a miracle!

I fasted and prayed for ten days.

One day, quite unexpectedly, there was a knock on my door. I opened the door, and there was a well-dressed lady standing before me. She told me her name and explained that her husband was the Vice-President of the Bank of Athens and that she had come to help me.

The Day God Rained 'Manna' From Heaven To Meet Our Needs

She shared with me the events that had just recently transpired that had changed the course of her life. Just two weeks prior to my arrival, as she was walking down the street, she heard music coming from a room on the second floor in one of the buildings.

She ventured up the stairway into a small room where a little group of Foursquare people had assembled for a midweek service. There, she surrendered her heart to the Lord Jesus Christ and was born again.

During the days that followed her experience in that small room, she learned that I had come from America to hold miracle services. She told me that she was going to ask her husband to use all of his influence to make it possible to conduct our meeting.

In less than two days, her husband had met with the prime minister and had made all the necessary arrangements to conduct the meeting.

The greatest miracle in the history of Greece since the Early Church took place! We secured permits to rent a building, to print and distribute handbills, and to buy ads in the newspapers. We were able to put the whole meeting together in just a few days' time.

The night of the meeting came, and we had only one problem left to solve: we needed an interpreter. I had no one.

As we were preparing for the meeting that night, I received a telephone call in my hotel room at 6 p.m., one hour before the meeting was to begin. The man on the other end of the line asked, "Is this Dr. Cerullo?" I answered, "Yes, who is this?"

"You don't know me, but I am your interpreter," came the reply.

I was taken by surprise, "Who are you?"

He answered, "I am Reverend Frangus, General Superintendent of all the Assemblies of God work in Greece. No one expected me, I'm just here by accident." (He was on a field missionary trip.)

"I called our missionary in Athens, and she told me that you were conducting services and that you needed an interpreter. I just want you to know I am rushing to the auditorium right now."

Believe me, I knew he wasn't there by accident. God had arranged it all! The night I was to open the meeting, God gave me the best interpreter I could ever have.

God blessed in a great way during that crusade. The very first night the place was packed, and every night 90 % of the audience stood up to receive Jesus Christ as their Savior.

God began moving with miracle after miracle. They couldn't get into the auditorium, so the people lined the streets with stretchers, wheelchairs, the blind, the lame, and the sick. They were so anxious for God to work a miracle in their lives.

As the time approached for us to close the meeting, Reverend Frangus came to see me. He said "Brother Cerullo, you can't close this meeting."

I knew how they felt, and I didn't want to close the meeting either. But because of the restrictions placed upon me, I had not been able to take any offerings to pay for the expenses. We had been given a permit for everything except to take offerings.

I was flat broke. I had spent the little money I had brought with me to pay for the advertisement, the handbills, and the rent on the building every night. I didn't even have enough money to go on to Israel as I had planned.

I told them, "I'm sorry, tomorrow night I must close the meeting."

I suggested to Brother Frangus that he try to call his headquarters and get a few thousand dollars to keep the meeting going. He explained to me that by the time it would take for his request to go through all the necessary red tape, it would be too late.

The Day God Rained 'Manna' From Heaven To Meet Our Needs

That night when, I returned to my room, I began to pray:

"Lord, You hear what these ministers are asking me. They have told me of the stripes on their backs that they have received for the sake of the Gospel. Now the freedom is here. Lord, they don't want this meeting to close. I don't want it to close, but I don't know what to do!"

Guess what the Lord said to me in prayer? He said to me, "Son, you've got the money."

"Oh, boy, this is wonderful," I said, "I've got the money!"

"Lord, do You mind telling me where I've got the money? If You tell me where it is, I'll go get it."

God answered me by saying, "You've got it at home."

I thought to myself, No, You wouldn't ask that. Surely You are not asking me to give the money that Theresa and I have in the bank for our little dream house.

I said, "Lord, I can't do that. I can do a lot of things, but I can't do that. That has to be Theresa's decision."

I called Theresa and told her how God was working in the lives of the people, performing miracle after miracle, and how many souls were being won into the Kingdom of God. I said, "Darling, I can't go on with the meeting. I don't have any more money."

She said to me, "Sweetheart, I know why you're calling. You want me to take the money for our new house and send it to you."

I said, "I didn't ask."

She replied, "You didn't have to ask. I'll send it to you."

Theresa withdrew our savings from the bank and wired it to me. It was enough to continue the meetings. And, after obtaining permission, the meetings continued on, night after night, with large crowds and God blessing in a mighty way.

I used a little of the savings to go on to Israel, as I had planned. It was a mountaintop experience as I stood in Israel and looked out over the nation for the very first time in my life. I knew, deep within, one day I would be back.

Arriving at New York International, I left the plane to find Theresa, David, and Susan waiting. The first thing I did was reach in my pocket, take out the small amount of change, and then I pulled out my empty pockets as I walked toward Theresa and the children. Reaching them, I held out my hand with the few coins, "This is it, the only thing between us and starvation!"

We had lost our house and also the deposit on the house. I set out once again, preaching and touring, with Theresa and the children accompanying me. The Lord blessed us during the next year with the same amount of savings it had previously taken us four years to accumulate. Isn't God good?

One day, while we were back at Theresa's parents' home, I said, "Theresa, you know, we should go look in the development where we were going to buy a home. We've got enough to buy or build again. Let's go see if there isn't another lot in that area."

As we drove into the development, located in a beautiful wooded area, we passed by "our house," the one we had lost. Lo and behold, in the front yard was a "For Sale" sign!

"Well, would you believe that, after a year!" I exclaimed. "Honey, let's go see Jeff and ask about it."

We drove to see Jeff Baron, the real estate salesman and friend of ours who had originally sold the house to us.

The Day God Rained 'Manna' From Heaven To Meet Our Needs

"Jeff, I see my old house is for sale. What are they asking for it?"

Jeff looked at us and smiled, "That house, it's the worst mover we have. I've got houses selling right and left all around it, but that house, we can't sell it!"

"What do you mean?"

"That house has been vacant for a whole year, ever since you built it."

"You mean you've never sold it?"

"No. We've sold all around it, same builder, all over the development, but that house, no one wants it."

"Jeff," I looked him straight in the eye, "how would you like to get rid of that lemon?"

We talked for a few minutes, then Jeff said, "Look, tell you what I'll do. If you're interested in buying the house, I'll go back to the owners and see what they will do. The houses have gone up in price about $3,000."

Jeff called me: "Dr. Cerullo, do you know what? I can't believe it, but the developers said that if you want the house, they will sell it to you for the old price that you built it for a year ago. Plus, they will even give you back your $600 deposit you lost last year when you couldn't go through with the deal."

Theresa and I rejoiced as we moved into our first little house, realizing that God had saved it for us. The very thing we sacrificed, God gave back to us!

Through this experience we learned a very valuable lesson. You just can't out give or out sacrifice God. And, He will open up the "windows" of heaven to provide for our needs when we come to Him in simple loyalty to His Word. There are many, other instances Theresa and I could share with you about how God has provided for our needs.

God does not change. He has made miracle provisions for you and your family. Don't ever think for even one moment that God is not concerned about your financial needs. He is!

He knows the anxiety you feel when the bills keep piling up, or when things feel a little shaky on your job, and you don't know how long your job is going to last.

Even when you are facing difficult circumstances, like Theresa and I faced when we didn't know where our next penny was coming from, keep your eyes on a miracle-working God, and He will never let you down. The Bible says to prove Him and see if He will not open up the windows of heaven and pour you out such a blessing you will not be able to receive it (Malachi 3:10).

Chapter Eleven

The Miracle In Haiti

Since my first overseas crusade in Athens, Greece, 52 years ago, I have been around the world many times ministering God's Word, training Nationals, and praying for the sick. God has greatly blessed, as multiplied thousands have accepted Jesus Christ as their Savior. Miracles of healing and deliverance have taken place in meeting after meeting. There have been some services when as many as 30 deaf and mute people have been healed at one time.

But with these great victories, I have also experienced many spiritual battles. I have faced almost every discouraging circumstance imaginable. I was arrested in Argentina on two different occasions for preaching the Gospel. I have been taken at gunpoint and questioned by Nicaraguan soldiers. I have preached two or three hours in a great downpour of rain until the water was ankle deep. I have preached while tanks roared down the streets of Porto Alegre, Brazil. On one occasion in Argentina the police barricaded the streets to hold back the 30,000 to 40,000 people who were trying to enter the stadium where we were scheduled to conduct a meeting.

I realize that most people in their lifetime will not face these same type of circumstances. But, it is possible that the circumstances you face on your job or in your family at times seem just as frightening or desperate to you as if you were looking down the barrel of a loaded gun.

God has been faithful to me. He has made me more than a conqueror and continues to give me victory in every circumstance I face. That is why I can encourage you to believe God for a miracle regarding the circumstances in your life.

The Miracle Book

There is one very unforgettable experience when my life was in danger, and God miraculously intervened. He revealed a plot to kill me, delivered me out of their hands, and proved to all those present that He was the only true and living God!

This particular miracle centers around a crusade in 1960 on the island of Haiti. I had gone there to hold a five-day crusade in connection with the Full Gospel Business Men's Fellowship International Convention.

I arrived during a celebration that was very similar to our Mardi Gras, which continued seven Sundays in a row. On the last day of this celebration, anything goes. They claim five thousand girls in one night are raped on the streets. Drunkenness, vileness, and witchcraft are all included.

During these days of celebration, our posters advertising the crusade were posted all over the island. I did not know, as I approached this island by plane, that these posters with my picture on them were being torn down by the witch doctors and were being burned. Other posters were found with pins sticking in my picture.

I was met at the airport by high-ranking officials and limousines. They had planned to have a motorcade through the city which would pass by the president's house.

On the way, I became so sick that I said to my soloist at that time, "Swen, if you don't mind, please help me. I want to go to my hotel. I don't want to go in this motorcade."

Upon arriving at the hotel, I got up to my room, fell down on my knees, and started to pray, "Lord, what is it? What do I feel inside me?"

"Son, this is not a physical sickness but a spiritual discernment that I have allowed. Tonight there is going to be trouble."

"What is it, Lord?"

148

"There are hundreds of witch doctors who are already mad at you. They are coming to kill you. They have organized and are going to break up the meeting."

I said, "Well, now, Lord, I'm glad that You told me. If I am supposed to die, fine. I'll be a martyr for Your sake." (I have had to say this more than once in my life. On many occasions I have had to face audiences knowing that I might be killed.)

"If this is what you want, it is all right with me. But what should I do?"

God said to me (the only time He ever said this to me in my life), "Son, the word that you speak will be exactly as if I had spoken it, and that word will come to pass."

How do you cope with knowing that you have in your ability the power of life and death?

I went to that service that night. Two hundred dignitaries flooded that platform. They filled every chair. There were senators and generals on the platform who had been given directives to come to the meeting. Five thousand people were jammed up against the platform. There were about 10,000 people in the bleachers, 15,000 people out the first night, and it was havoc. People were laughing, jeering, and mocking. It was a mess.

When I was introduced, it was a little bit quieter and calmer, and I greeted the people. Then, suddenly, it started. Throughout the congregation, in little groups scattered here and there, the witch doctors started chanting. There were hundreds and hundreds of witch doctors there. I thought we were going to have a riot. Noisy mumbling would start up in front. Then another group would start somewhere else. The atmosphere was charged with fear. Those on the platform behind me looked scared and worried, fearful of a riot.

I called for quiet.

They started the chanting again, a second time, and I called for quiet. They did it a third time, and I once again called for quiet.

The fourth time I said, "All right, this is the last time I am going to speak. I have asked for reverence and quiet three times now to be able to give you God's Word. I want you to know that I didn't just decide to come to Haiti. God sent me here. The true and living God sent me to you. He gave me a message of love. He gave me a message of healing for you. He loves you. He wants to save you. He wants to forgive your sins, bless you, and heal you. Now that is the message He sent me here to bring to you. But, that God is also a God of judgment.

"Today, in my room, God showed me that there were hundreds of witch doctors who would be here tonight to destroy this meeting. I am going to be here in this city for some time. We had better find out tonight, this first night, whether you and your devil have more power than me and my God!

"Now, (and I turned around and looked at all those dignitaries), I serve notice that I take no responsibility for what happens from this point on. The NEXT PERSON IN THIS STADIUM who opens their mouth, and says one word to hinder or to destroy this meeting, I will take no responsibility before all these individuals on the platform when they carry you out of this stadium DEAD!"

That whole group got so quiet you could hear a pin drop. I never had one more bit of trouble. I only preached about 15 or 20 minutes, when suddenly, from the back of that large congregation, someone began to scream. They began to push a little baby over the top of everyone's head. I said to my interpreter, "What is going on?"

He said, "Brother Cerullo, while you were preaching, a child back there, who was born blind, can now see and is grabbing for his parent's eyes, nose, ears, and head. The place is going wild."

Finally, they got the little child to the platform. Her parents pushed through to the front and began testing the child to show she had sight.

Suddenly, a high-ranking Haitian official, wearing a uniform with many bars and gold braids, stood up. "My God!" he exclaimed excitedly, "That's my neighbor's child."

As a result of this tremendous miracle in the life of a little three-year-old child, scores of witch doctors were converted to Christ that night.

On the second night of the meeting, God proved to the Haitian people that He is the true God Who has power over the laws of nature. Dark clouds filled the sky, and it looked as if it would begin to rain at any moment.

The Haitians are very superstitious. They believe that if they are rained upon, it is a sign of bad luck. Not wanting to be rained upon, people began to run out of the meeting. "In the Name of Jesus, I command you to stop running and stand still." The words spewed forth from my mouth with a special anointing of power and authority from God.

The people stopped running.

"In the Name of Jesus, turn around and look at me. You see those dark clouds? Now you are going to know what kind of prophet of God I am. It will not rain."

After this statement, we continued the meeting for another hour and a half.

Then I turned to the audience and said. "The service is over. After I pray you must get home quickly because it's going to rain."

About ten minutes after they started out of that place, it started raining. God confirmed the words He had given me to speak.

The meeting lasted three weeks instead of five days. The crowds grew to 35,000. Thousands were saved and healed. From the first night forward, scores of witch doctors were saved! During the three weeks, thousands of fetishes were brought and piled on the altar.

One evening, during the middle of the first week, several people connected with the crusade and I went to the house of the leading witch doctor. This witch doctor and his entire family had been marvelously converted to Jesus Christ during the crusade. We tore everything associated with witchcraft and the occult down from his walls and carried it out of his house, taking it to the middle of the street. Then, we set it afire!

Excitement and joy filled the street and overflowed into the neighborhood as we celebrated God's victory. We marched around and around that bonfire singing at the top of our voices: "What can wash away my sins? Nothing but the Blood of Jesus!"

Seeing lives, such as these witch doctors and thousands of others from every nationality and walk of life, transformed by the power of God is what keeps me going year after year to the nations of the world. I could go on crusade after crusade, ministering seven days a week, 30 days a month, month after month, as long as I see what God is doing in the lives of people down at the altar.

What a thrill it is for me to watch as God performs miracles in service after service, as He confirms His Word and meets the needs of people.

I cannot describe to you the joy that floods my being as I watch the expression on the faces of those who have been healed by the power of God.

How can I forget the excitement and joy that spreads across the face of a young child, who has lived in a silent world for years, when he suddenly realizes he can hear? Or, the tears of joy that flood the face of a mother who hears her child (who was a deaf-mute) say "Mama" for the first time in her life? How can I forget the beaming faces of those who have been delivered, set free, from the living nightmare of years spent in bondage to alcohol and drugs?

I cannot and will not forget. I will continue to go. I will continue to believe. I will continue to tell others about a miracle-working God. I will continue to expect miracles to be performed in the lives of people everywhere.

God is not limited by the laws of nature. He is unlimited, all powerful. Just as He caused the rain not to fall in Haiti, God can speak to whatever need you have right now. He wants you to realize that you are not alone. He has promised to be with you...*Fear not: for I have redeemed thee, I have called thee by thy name; thou art mine. When thou passest through the waters, I will be with thee; and through the rivers, they shall not overflow thee: when thou walkest through the fire, thou shalt not be burned; neither shall the flame kindle upon thee* (Isaiah 43:1-2).

The God we serve is a God of purpose, plan, design, and objectivity.

Nothing in life happens by accident.

God is in control of the circumstances in your life. His purpose and His Will for you is that you experience a breakthrough into a new spiritual dimension that will enable you to live your life in a rhythm of daily victory miracle living.

God is concerned about you. Keep your eyes off your circumstances, receive the Word into your spirit, and believe God for a miracle.

The Miracle Book

Chapter Twelve

We Haven't Seen Anything Yet!

In 1959, when I was just a young man of 27, God sent me to the Philippine Islands.

We were in the Roxas Park, across the street from the city hall in Manila, for three weeks in a crusade. God was doing so many wonderful things. On the last day of the crusade, we had a water baptismal service with over 50 National ministers baptizing more than 1,200 people who had given their lives to Jesus. Tens of thousands had made decisions for Christ, but we were able to process only about 1,200 of them in one mass baptismal service in Manila Bay.

We returned to Roxas Park with about 30,000 people present for the closing afternoon service.

I began to minister, and had talked only for about ten minutes, when suddenly, something began to happen to a man who was in one of the worst, most hopeless conditions I have ever seen in my life. He was so twisted, he was rolled up in a ball lying on the ground. This man was just one of hundreds and hundreds of cripples, blind, deaf, and maimed lying all over the place in this crusade, waiting to be touched by the healing power of our blessed Lord and Savior, Jesus Christ.

As I continued to bring the message, that man who was so crippled and twisted started to move. I will never forget him as long as I live. He started to stretch out and untwist first his legs, and then his arms. Then he got up! You could hear his bones cracking as his limbs twisted into their proper shape. That man ran across the front of the roped area, leaping and shouting, and suddenly that whole service became spiritual bedlam. I couldn't control it.

I saw mothers-not one, but dozens-take their little children and tear the braces off their legs. They would take their little children, stand them up on their feet, and say, "Walk, in the Name of Jesus!"

I would see dozens of those little children just fall right to the ground, crumpled in a heap because their feet were like rubber, and they could not stand. I watched those Filipinos take the little babies up again and command, "I said walk, in the Name of Jesus!"

Some fell three times, some four, again and again and again and again, until you saw little children running here and running there, and crutches went flying. There were dozens of walking sticks, canes, and crutches thrown up on the platform in just a few minutes' time.

Do you know what happened to me, when I saw these tremendous manifestations of God's power?

I ran. I ran because I was afraid. There was a big post behind the platform, and I hid behind it.

A big, tall missionary came over to me, put his arms around me, and said, "Brother Cerullo, you better get back to the rostrum, or we are going to have a riot on our hands. You are the only person who can hold this meeting in order."

I went back to the platform, and I saw people running here, running there, crutches flying, walking sticks flying, little babies falling, and little babies walking. I was weeping like a little child.

I said to God, "God, no one should ever see this much of Your glory and be allowed to live. God, take me home. I want to die."

Then God spoke something to me I have never forgotten.
He said to me, "Son, you haven't seen anything yet!"

I have seen many mighty miracles of God since that time, but God is still speaking to my heart that we haven't seen anything yet.

If only we could see God as He really is. If only we could realize that there is no such thing as a day of miracles, but there is a miracle-working God in our midst every day. He does not change.

I believe in a miracle-working God Who wants us to be His people of miracles. He wants His miracle-working power to be a flow and a rhythm in our lives all the time. He wants us to be living, walking extensions of His miracle ability.

Believing God for a miracle in your life may be a new experience for you. Or, you may have been patiently waiting upon God for the manifestation of a miracle in your life for many years.

Whatever the case may be, I urge you to break out of your environment. There are no impossibilities with God. Determine in your heart to take every limitation off God and allow Him to reveal Himself to you in a greater way than you ever dreamed possible.

Begin to recognize God as your heavenly Father Who is interested in every area of your life. Run to Him in times of need as your children run to you for help, comfort, security, and love. Don't be afraid to share even the smallest details of your life. He created you for His pleasure. He enjoys the time that you take to fellowship with Him.

I believe God has a purpose, plan, and objective for everything He does. He has a purpose for you reading this book. I believe He wants you to know that He has so much more that He wants to accomplish in your life, if you will let Him.

Friend, you haven't seen anything yet!

From this day forward, God wants you to experience and live in a new awareness of His miracle-working power. Begin to think in terms of miracles. Miracles are not meant to be the exception in your life.

Miracles are the rule, because you serve a miracle-working God Who manifests Himself through miracles.

Throughout this book, I have given you a glimpse into my life. I have shown you how God took me, as a small orphan boy-who knew about God but did not really know Him personally-and taught me through the circumstances that came into my life how to live a life filled with miracles.

I did not receive an instantaneous revelation of the possibilities of living in a rhythm of miracles.

God took me one step at a time, and, it was not easy. There were times I felt alone, misunderstood, and desperate to receive an answer from God.

I have not written a theological dissertation to prove to you that miracles are possible. The Living Word of God within every born-again believer is proof enough! The five steps I have presented to you are based on the Word of God. I am believing His Word will become firmly planted within your spirit, and as it does, I know it will produce God's purpose for your life, a new day-to-day experience with a God Who is and always will be a miracle-working God.

Hear God's Word…,Receive it…,Act on it.

A miracle-something which cannot happen by human means- is waiting for you.

Chapter Thirteen

The Greatest Miracle Of All

Throughout my fifty-three years of ministry, in more than 130 countries of the world, I have witnessed God work multiplied thousands of miracles of all kinds: Blind eyes have been opened; deaf ears have been unstopped; crippled, deformed limbs have been restored; cancer and all types of sickness and diseases have been healed.

I will never forget the many manifestations of God's power and glory as He has reached down and delivered people of all ages and races from the terrible bondage of sickness and disease.

I am an eyewitness to the fact that there is no limit to His miracle-working power!

However, the healing of blindness, deafness, heart disease or cancer is not the greatest miracle in the world.

All of these manifestations are awe inspiring, and we praise God for them.

Without a doubt the greatest miracle in the world is the healing of a person's soul.

But, the awesome healing and transformation of man's soul did not come without a price.

The *ultimate* price was paid to cleanse man from his sins and to restore us to fellowship with God.

When God created Adam and Eve and placed them in the beautiful Garden of Eden, He intended them to be His children with whom He would have intimate fellowship.

God created them in His own image, *"And God said, let us make man in our image, after our likeness: and let them have dominion over the fish of the sea, and over the fowl of the air, and over the cattle, and over the earth, and over every creeping thing that creepeth upon the earth."* (Genesis 1:26)

God breathed His life into Adam and Eve and they became living *souls*. God did not want man to be like a puppet on a string. He did not want forced fellowship. He did not want Adam and Eve to be forced to love Him. He gave them a *will*.

To find the Image of God in man, one must go beneath the outward exterior to the very core of man's being. There, with all the temporal things in the background, we find the soul and spirit. It is there that we find the image of God.

It is the power God gave man to be one of His sons.

It is the power of your will! God gave you this gift as you were created in His image.

God gave man dominion over the earth and everything in it. One of the first things He did was to command His blessing upon Adam and Eve. *"And God blessed them and God said unto them, "Be fruitful, and multiply, and replenish the earth, and subdue it: and have dominion over the fish of the sea, and over the fowl of the air, and over every living thing that moveth upon the earth."* (Genesis 1:28)

Adam and Eve were created in the image of God—-perfect. They had everything they needed. There was no sin, sickness or disease. They lived in a perfect environment in full fellowship with God. As their Father, He came down and walked and talked with them in the cool of the day. Everything they needed was given to them to enjoy.

God never intended for man to know pain, sickness or disease. He never intended for man to live in a world plagued with wars, murder, rape, fear, turmoil, Aids, cancer and other debilitating diseases.

He never intended for us to die!

The questions arise: Why do we become sick? Why do we sin? Why do we die?

Adam and Eve disobeyed God's commandment—they rebelled against God. As a result, they lost their position of power and dominion over the earth. But, more importantly, they forfeited their close intimate fellowship with God.

God told them: *"You are free to eat from any tree in the garden; but you must not eat from the tree of the knowledge of good and evil, for when you eat of it you will surely die."* (Genesis 2:15-17, NIV)

Man had within him the free will to obey or disobey.

Adam and Eve were faced with a decision – to do good and obey God, or to do evil and obey Satan.

Every power on earth falls into one of two categories: the power of God or the power of the devil. You may classify them as the power of good and the power of evil, the power of life or the power of death.

"The thief cometh not, but for to steal, and to kill, and to destroy: I am come that they might have life and that they might have it more abundantly." (John 10:10)

Satan came to Adam and Eve in the Garden of Eden and tempted them. First, he questioned what God had told them. *"Can it really be that God has said, You shall not eat of every tree of the garden?"* (Genesis 3:1, AMP)

Eve answered that they were allowed to eat fruit from any of the trees in the garden except for the tree in the middle of the garden. She said, *"God has said, You shall not eat of it, neither shall you touch it, lest you die."* (Genesis 3:3, AMP)

Satan challenged God's command and warning to Adam and Eve. He subtly deceived Eve into thinking that the fruit would make them wise, like God. He said, "You surely shall not die! For God knows that in the day you eat from it your eyes will be opened, and you will be like God, knowing good and evil." (Genesis 3:4-5, NAS)

One of the major contributing factors that led to their sin was the fact that instead of rejecting Satan's lies, she listened to him. As she looked upon the fruit and saw how beautiful it was and that it would make her wise, she yielded to temptation. She took of the fruit, ate it and gave some to Adam, who also at the fruit.

Immediately, their eyes were opened. "Then the eyes of both of them were opened, and they realized they were naked; so they sewed fig leaves together and made coverings for themselves. As a result of their sin, they became afraid and tried to hide from God."

The Lord called Adam and said, "Where are you"?

Adam answered, *"I heard you in the garden, and I was afraid because I was naked; so I hid."* (Genesis 3:10, NIV)

Adam told God, *"The woman you put here with me – she gave me some fruit from the tree, and I ate it."* (Genesis 3:12, NIV)

"What is this that you have done? God asked Eve.
Eve replied, *"The serpent deceived me, and I ate."* (Genesis 3:13, NIV)

God Sent His Son For A Divine Purpose

The devil influenced Adam and Eve and caused them to disobey God. By their disobedience in partaking of the tree of knowledge of good and evil, they brought sin into the world… and through sin, sickness… and, death. That is how sin, sickness and death came into the world.

"Wherefore, as by one man sin entered into the world, and death by sin; and so death passed upon all men, for that all have sinned." (Romans 5:12)

Adam and Eve received the penalty of their sin. God released a curse upon them. But first, He pronounced a curse upon the devil, represented by the serpent. He said, *"Because you have done this, cursed are you above all the livestock and all the wild animals! You will crawl on your belly and you will eat dust all the days of your life. And I will put enmity between you and the woman, and between your offspring and hers; he will crush your head, and you will strike his heel."* (Genesis 3:14-15, NIV)

One day there would come from the seed of a woman, the perfect Sacrifice for sin that would, once and for all, bruise the head of Satan. One day Satan's power would be stripped from him and God would return to man the authority that he originally had.

Through Adam and Eve's disobedience, man came under a curse. That curse brought sin, sickness and death.

God told Eve, *"I will greatly increase your pains in childbearing; with pain you will give birth to children. Your desire will be for your husband, and he will rule over you."* (Genesis 3:16, NIV)

God told Adam, *"Cursed is the ground because of you; through painful toil you will eat of it all the days of your life. It will produce thorns and thistles for you and you will eat the plants of the field. By the sweat of your brow you will eat your food until you return to the ground, since from it you were taken; for dust you are and to dust you will return."* (Genesis 3:17-19, NIV)

But, God's love for mankind was so great He did not leave man in his sin and disobedience. God made a master plan whereby He would break the curse of sin, sickness and death and restore man to fellowship with Him to an even greater place of intimacy. Restoration!

How? God paid the ultimate price to redeem mankind.

What was the ultimate price?

His only son.

"For God so loved the world that He gave His only begotten son that whosoever believeth in Him should not perish, but have everlasting life." (John 3:16)

Two thousand years ago God sent His only Son into the world for a divine purpose.

The Apostle John said, *"In the beginning was the Word, and the Word was with God, and the Word was God. The same was in the beginning with God. All things were made by him; and without him was not anything made that was made. And the Word was made flesh, and dwelt among us (and we beheld his glory, the glory as of the only begotten of the Father,) full of grace and truth."* (John 1:1-3, 14)

The Son of God, who was with God from the beginning of time, took upon Himself the form of a man with flesh and blood, arms, legs, and eyes like you and me.

The eternal God of the universe subjected Himself to the frailties and the temptations of man. In the form of man, He lived a sinless life. *"For we have not an high priest which cannot be touched with the feeling of our infirmities; but was in all points tempted like as we are, yet without sin."* (Hebrews 4:15)

Jesus Came To Break The Curse Of Sin

Jesus, the Son of God, became like you and me, that He might lift us out of our sins and restore us into fellowship with the Father. His purpose was to remove the curse and separation of sin and to destroy all the works of the devil.

"...For this purpose the Son of God was manifested, that he might destroy the works of the devil." (1 John 3:8)

Jesus did not come to wound the devil but to literally destroy his power over your life. He came to destroy the works of the Devil. The word "destroy" in this verse is from a Greek word meaning, "To put out of action. To make useless!"

Jesus did not come to sit on a throne and wear a crown of diamonds on his head. He did not come to rule as a king over man. He came to set men free from all the power of Satan.

While He lived upon this earth, Jesus fulfilled the will of the Father. He opened blind eyes, opened deaf ears, healed the lame and all kinds of sickness and disease, cast out devils and raised the dead.

Jesus came to lay down His life as the only sacrifice sufficient to redeem mankind. He was the Lamb of God *"slain from the foundation of the world."* (Revelation 13:8) He was willing to give His life that you and I might have eternal life and be free from all evil.

God's master plan of redemption required the sacrifice of His most prized possession…His only Son. *"…without the shedding of blood is no remission."* (Hebrews 9:22) Our redemption called for Jesus to shed His blood and give His life.

No man took Jesus' life from Him. He willingly laid it down on the cross. When the soldiers came to arrest Him, He said, *"Thinkest thou that I cannot now pray to my Father, and he shall presently give more than twelve legions of angels? But how then shall the scriptures be fulfilled, that thus it must be?"* (Matthew 26:53-54)

The Roman soldiers stripped the clothes off His back and strapped Him to the whipping post. They beat him with a whip made of many leather straps and bits of metal until His back was laid bare.

They mocked and ridiculed Him.

They shoved a crown of thorns on His head until blood poured down His face.

The cruel Roman soldiers beat Him and pulled out His beard until His face was almost unrecognizable. Hundreds of years earlier the prophet Isaiah prophesied concerning Christ's sufferings, *"his appearance was disfigured beyond that of any man and his form marred beyond human likeness."* (Isaiah 52:14)

Isaiah prophesied that He would be despised and rejected and bear our sins, sicknesses and sorrow upon Himself. "He is despised and rejected of men; a man of sorrows, and acquainted with grief: and we hid as it were our faces from him; he was despised, and we esteemed him not. Surely he hath borne our griefs, and carried our sorrows: yet we did not esteem him stricken, smitten of God, afflicted. But he was wounded for our transgressions, he was bruised for our iniquities: the chastisement of our peace was upon him; and with his stripes we are healed." (Isaiah 53:1-5)

"It Is Finished!"

Christ was nailed to a Roman cross and crucified between two thieves. They pierced His side and the blood flowed forth. As He hung there, the blood flowed from His hands and feet. Your sins and mine were nailed to the cross that day!

He took our sicknesses upon Himself and with His stripes, we are healed. *"He himself bore our sins in his body on the tree, so that we might die to sins and live for righteousness; by his wounds you have been healed."* (1 Peter 2:24, NIV)

Can you see Him there, the eternal Son of God, hanging in shame and disgrace, carrying the weight of the sins and sicknesses of the world upon Himself?

Jesus lifted His eyes toward Heaven and said, *"Father, forgive them: for they know not what they do."* (Luke 23:34) The price had been paid. Forgiveness and restoration of man to the Father was purchased that day as He hung there on the cross.

Knowing that He had fulfilled His Father's will, Jesus cried out, *"It is finished!"* (John 19:30)

"It is finished!" The three most powerful words ever spoken. God's plan of redemption was forever accomplished. There is nothing man can ever do to earn his own salvation. A person doesn't have to struggle to "clean up his act" before coming to God.

Jesus paid the price!

It is finished!

Through His death on the cross, Jesus destroyed the works of Satan and broke his power over mankind. *"Forasmuch then as the children are partakers of flesh and blood, he also himself likewise took part of the same; that through death he might destroy him that had the power of death, that is the devil; And deliver them who through fear of death were all their lifetime subject to bondage."* (Hebrews 2:14-15)

Man is no longer bound by sin, sickness or death!

Jesus broke the bondage of death. They took Him and laid His body in the grave. But the grave could not hold Him.

Death could not keep Him!

On the third day, He arose triumphant over the grave.

Jesus Christ was not just a prophet or teacher.

He is the Son of the living God. He is alive forever more! He ascended into heaven where He is now seated in a position of supreme power and authority over all power and principalities in heaven and on earth!

Satan's bondage on mankind has forever been destroyed. Christ holds the keys of hell and death. Jesus said, *"I am he that liveth, and was dead; and behold, I am alive for evermore, Amen; and have the keys of hell and death."* (Revelation 1:18)

What Does This Mean To You?

God loves you just as you are. He loved you so much that He paid the ultimate price for you to be redeemed and restored into fellowship with Him as one of His children.

God does not want to be a mystery...a powerful Being that cannot be understood, that cannot be reached. He has provided a way that you can come to Him and know Him intimately. His desire is that you will make Him part of your life, sharing your joys and accomplishments as well as your disappointments and heartaches.

He feels our pain and sorrow even more than we do because He has already spoken the word that will meet every circumstance and every need.

Yet, man refuses to come to Him.

Oh, that men everywhere would open their eyes and get a clear glimpse of God as He really is!

A Sixth Sense

God has not made it a difficult, complicated procedure to reach Him, to know Him, to see Him as He is. There are no rigid requirements for an individual to meet. Man does not have to change before he comes to God. The change will come after he meets God.

There is only one way man can have God revealed to him. He cannot see and know God through his intellect. It is impossible. The natural mind is incapable of comprehending His greatness. God has made this clear in His Word: *"But the natural man receiveth not the things of the Spirit of God: for they are foolishness unto him: neither can he know them, because they are spiritually discerned."* (1 Corinthians 2:14)

Neither can man reach God through his good works (Ephesians 2:8-9). If he tries any other way than the way God has directed, he is fooling himself.

There is only one way.

Jesus said, "I am the way, the truth, and the life: no man cometh unto the Father, but by me:" (John 14:6)

The only way man can see God as He is revealed through His Son, Jesus Christ. As an individual comes to Jesus, surrenders his will and accepts Christ into his life, the greatest of all miracles happens. He is born again!

He becomes a new person with new desires and a new spiritual mind. *"Therefore if any man be in Christ, he is a new creature: old things are passed away; behold, all things are become new."* (2 Corinthians 5:17)

The Spirit of God is supernaturally implanted in him. So then they that are in the flesh cannot please God. *"But ye are not in the flesh, but in the Spirit, if so be that the Spirit of God dwell in you. Now if any man have not the Spirit of Christ, he is none of his."* (Romans 8:8-9)

Through the Spirit of God, it is possible to see God and to know the miracle provisions He has made for you. *"That the God of our Lord Jesus Christ, the Father of glory, may give unto you the spirit of wisdom and revelation in the knowledge of him: The eyes of your understanding being enlightened; that ye may know what is the hope of his calling, and what the riches of the glory of his inheritance in the saints."* (Ephesians 1:17-18)

God has provided a way whereby any man...no matter who he may be, no matter what he may have done, regardless of his nationality or status in life...can have access to Him and have his needs met.

Man has been given five natural senses: we see, we hear, we taste, we smell, we touch. However, man cannot reach God through these natural senses.

Why?

Because God is supernatural and man cannot reach Him through natural means. In order to reach God, He has provided a sixth sense for all that accepts Jesus Christ as Lord and Savior and surrenders their lives to Him. It is a supernatural sense because it is not the product of man.

When an individual is spiritually born again he receives a new sixth sense, which he did not possess when he was born with his five natural senses. This sixth sense is called faith.

Some people feel that they must struggle to produce faith before they receive anything from God. They try to use the power of positive thinking or scripture memorization in an effort to produce faith. The power of positive thinking cannot produce faith. Scripture memorization cannot produce faith.

Man does not need to struggle. No matter how hard he may try, man cannot produce faith. It is not a natural life-force.

It is a gift of God that man receives when he accepts Christ into his life. With Jesus comes faith. *"For by grace are ye saved through faith; and that not of yourselves: it is the gift of God: Not of works, lest any man should boast."* (Ephesians 2:8-9)

Reach Out And Accept Christ Today!

Friend, God has a purpose for your life. Regardless of who you are, where you have been, or what you have done, He *loves* you!

Jesus Christ came to restore you to fellowship with God. His purpose for your life is that you be totally restored (made new), spirit, soul and body.

He came to give you life *more abundantly*. Jesus said, *"The thief cometh not, but for to steal, and to kill, and to destroy: I am come that they might have life, and that they might have it more abundantly."* (John 10:10)

If you are bound by habits, lustful desires, drugs or alcohol, He will deliver you.

If you are bound by fear, He will set you free.

If you are sick, He will heal you.

If you are reaching out for love, He will put His arms around you and fill you with *His* love.

God wants to set you free of every bondage the devil may try to place upon you.

God wants to speak peace into your life and make you 100 percent whole in every way.

The first thing you must do is to recognize you are a sinner and that you need a Savior. Through Adam's sin – disobedience against God, sin entered the world and, as a result, all men are born into this world with a sin nature. Sin is universal. *"For all have sinned, and come short of the glory of God".* (Romans 3:23)

Salvation is a gift. All men are given an opportunity to accept Christ and receive the greatest miracle of all – the salvation of their souls, or to reject Christ and live in their sins. It is God's will that all men accept Christ and be restored into fellowship with Him as their Father.

Today is the day of salvation.

You have a choice: To accept Christ and receive eternal life; or to refuse Christ and continue living your life your own way, following after your own desires and reap the wages of sin. *"For the wages of sin is death, but the gift of God is eternal life through Jesus Christ our Lord."* (Romans 3:23)

The second thing you must do to receive the greatest miracle of all is to surrender your will and life fully to God. This is the key. He alone can satisfy and fill the emptiness in your spirit. Jesus said, *"...and him that cometh to me I will in no wise cast out."* (John 6:37) He is waiting for you. Jesus said, *"Here I am! I stand at the door and knock. If anyone hears my voice and opens the door, I will come in and eat with him, and he with me."* (Revelation 3:20, NIV)

God is a Spirit and He is standing beside you right now. You cannot see Him, but He is there waiting for you to surrender your will and accept Christ as your Savior.

The third thing you do to receive the miracle of salvation is to confess your sins and turn away from them. God has given us this promise, *"If we confess our sins, he is faithful and just to forgive us our sins and to cleanse us from all unrighteousness."* (1 John 1:9)

You do not need to carry the weight of your past sins one minute longer. Regardless of what you may have done, Christ is ready to wipe the slate of your past clean. He is ready to forgive you of every sin you have ever committed and to remember it against you no more!

Once you have confessed your sins and accepted Christ as your Savior and Lord of your life, you need to seal it by making a confession of your faith in Jesus Christ.

> *"...if thou shalt confess with thy mouth the Lord Jesus, and shalt believe in thine heart that God hath raised him from the dead; thou shalt be saved. For with the heart man believeth unto righteousness: and with the mouth confession is made unto salvation."*
>
> Romans 10:9-10

Don't wait one minute longer. Pray this prayer aloud right now:

Dear Jesus,

I come to You, as I am...a sinner. I believe You are the Son of God, that You died on the cross, shed your blood for my sins and bore the stripes on your back for my healing.

I believe You rose from the dead and destroyed the power of Satan over my life.

I'm tired of going my way and "doing my thing." I surrender my life and will to You.

Right now, I repent of my sins. Forgive me, cleanse me and set me free from every sin. Deliver me from every habit that has me bound.

I accept you as my Lord and Savior. Fill me with Your Spirit, heal my soul and body and fill me with Your love, Your joy, Your peace.

Amen

Friend, praise God, you are now born again!

"...Truly, truly, I say to you, unless one is born anew, he cannot see the kingdom of God." (John 3:3, RSV)

You are a totally new person in Christ:

"Therefore, any one is in Christ, he is a new creation, the old has passed away, behold, the new has come." (2 Corinthians 5:17, RSV)

If you prayed this prayer and meant it from your heart, you have been set free of every sin! *"If therefore the Son shall make you free, you shall be free indeed."* (John 8:36, NIV)

You are a child of God and all His blessings belong to you.

The Miracle Book

It is important for you to know that you have just made the most important decision in your life.

The greatest of all miracles has happened to you. You are saved and are now a part of the family of God.

If you prayed this prayer and accepted Christ into your life, please fill out the Confession of Faith at the back of this book and send it to me so I can rejoice with you.

I want to pray for you and send you some important spiritual materials to help you in your new life.

God's Miracle Provision For You

Remember:
A miracle is something that cannot happen by human means. It is a supernatural intervention of God in the affairs of your life.

Follow the five steps:
1. See God As He Is;
2. Take Your Eyes Off Your Circumstances;
3. See Your Problems As Miracle Opportunities;
4. Realize In Every Promise Of God Is The Seed For Your Miracle;
5. Plant A Miracle Seed By Acting on God's Word.

Claim God's *miracle provisions.*

Salvation
If we confess our sins, he is faithful and just to forgive us our sins, and to cleanse us from all unrighteousness (I John 1:9).

For God so loved the world, that he gave his only begotten Son, that whosoever believeth in him should not perish, but have everlasting life (John 3:16).

...Believe on the Lord Jesus Christ, and thou shalt be saved, and thy house (Acts 16:31).

Bless the LORD, O my soul: and all that is within me, bless his holy name. Bless the LORD, O my soul, and forget not all his benefits: Who forgiveth all thine iniquities; who healeth all thy diseases; Who redeemeth thy life from destruction; who crowneth thee with lovingkindness and tender mercies; Who satisfieth thy mouth with good things; so that thy youth is renewed like the eagle's (Psalms 103:1-5).

The Miracle Book

Healing
But he was wounded for our transgressions, he was bruised for our iniquities: the chastisement of our peace was upon him; and with his stripes we are healed (Isaiah 53:5).

Who his own self bare our sins in his own body on the tree, that we, being dead to sins, should live unto righteousness: by whose stripes ye were healed (I Peter 2:24).

He sent his word, and healed them, and delivered them from their destructions (Psalm 107:20).

Deliverance
If the Son therefore shall make you free, ye shall be free indeed (John 8:36).

When thou passest through the waters, I will be with thee; and through the rivers, they shall not overflow thee: when thou walkest through the fire, thou shalt not be burned; neither shall the flame kindle upon thee (Isaiah 43:2).

Though I walk in the midst of trouble, thou wilt revive me: thou shalt stretch forth thine hand against the wrath of mine enemies, and thy right hand shall save me (Psalms 138:7).

Prosperity
And the LORD shall make thee plenteous in goods, in the fruit of thy body, and in the fruit of thy cattle, and in the fruit of thy ground, in the land which the LORD sware unto thy fathers to give thee. The LORD shall open unto thee his good treasure, the heaven to give the rain unto thy land in his season, and to bless all the work of thine hand: and thou shalt lend unto many nations, and thou shalt not borrow. And the LORD shall make thee the head, and not the tail; and thou shalt be above only, and thou shalt not be beneath; if that thou hearken unto the commandments of the LORD thy God, which I command thee this day, to observe and to do them (Deuteronomy 28:11-13).

And God is able to make all grace abound toward you; that ye, always having all sufficiency in all things, may abound to every good work (II Corinthians 9:8).

Give, and it shall be given unto you; good measure, pressed down, and shaken together, and running over, shall men give into your bosom. For with the same measure that ye mete withal it shall be measured to you again (Luke 6:38).

Guidance
Trust in the LORD with all thine heart; and lean not unto thine own understanding. In all thy ways acknowledge him, and he shall direct thy paths (Proverbs 3:5-6).

A man's heart deviseth his way: but the LORD directeth his steps (Proverbs 16:9).

I will instruct thee and teach thee in the way which thou shalt go: I will guide thee with mine eye (Psalms 32:8).

Strength
Wait on the LORD: be of good courage, and he shall strengthen thine heart: wait, I say, on the LORD (Psalms 27:14).

He giveth power to the faint; and to them that have no might he increaseth strength. Even the youths shall faint and be weary, and the young men shall utterly fall: But they that wait upon the LORD shall renew their strength; they shall mount up with wings as eagles; they shall run, and not be weary; and they shall walk, and not faint (Isaiah 40:29-31).

Though he fall, he shall not be utterly cast down: for the LORD upholdeth him with his hand

But the salvation of the righteous is of the LORD: he is their strength in the time of trouble (Psalms 37:24,39).

Peace

Thou wilt keep him in perfect peace, whose mind is stayed on thee: because he trusteth in thee (Isaiah 26:3).

And the peace of God, which passeth all understanding, shall keep your hearts and minds through Christ Jesus (Philippians 4:7).

I will both lay me down in peace, and sleep: for thou, LORD, only makest me dwell in safety (Psalms 4:8).

MORRIS CERULLO WORLD EVANGELISM

THE MAN...

Dr. Morris Cerullo, president of Morris Cerullo World Evangelism, is a man with a heart that beats for reaching and winning souls.

Out of more than 58 years of ministry, 56 years have been spent in worldwide evangelism, going to the nations and preaching and teaching a powerful, uncompromising message of salvation, healing and deliverance.

Thousands of Nationals worldwide have acknowledged Morris Cerullo as one of the leading prophets of the twenty first century. Not only does God speak to him, but his prophetic annunciations come with a special anointing of God's presence.

He received a divine, supernatural call from God to preach at the age of 15. From that time until now, he has never wavered in his commitment and zeal to fulfill the Great Commission to bring in a harvest of souls from around the world.

God has used Dr. Cerullo to pioneer overseas ministries, and to open many countries that have been considered closed to the Gospel. His ministry is accompanied by a manifestation of God's miracle-working power.

Many honors have been bestowed on Morris Cerullo, including honorary doctorates of divinity and humanities by academic and spiritual leaders and presidents of nations in recognition of his achievements and contributions to global evangelization.

Few ministers have had such an impact on the destiny of the nations of the world. Morris Cerullo's life has been sacrificially dedicated to training and spiritually equipping pastors, lay people, and evangelists to reach their nations for Christ with a supernatural endowment of God's power.

THE MESSAGE...

God has anointed Dr. Cerullo with a unique ability to communicate to others the power and anointing God has given him. The message he proclaims is the uncompromised Word of God on salvation, healing, baptism of the Holy Spirit, and Christ's second coming.

Over the past 58 years, God has used Morris to release prophetic messages over people and nations and to strengthen and prepare the Church to fulfill His purposes in this end-time hour.

He is one of the major leaders in the area of spiritual warfare. God has used his revolutionary messages on spiritual warfare to equip and train a vast army of spiritual warriors to move from a defensive to an offensive position and to walk in 100% victory in every area of their lives.

Breakthrough messages, such as *Proof Producers*, *The New Anointing*, *The Battle For Your Mind*, *The Last Great Anointing*, *The Battle For Your Tongue*, *Making Possible Your Impossibilities*, and many more, have revolutionized the lives of multiplied thousands worldwide.

THE MINISTRY...

Morris Cerullo World Evangelism is a cutting-edge ministry dedicated to training, equipping and building up the Body of Christ to do the work of the ministry.

SCHOOLS OF MINISTRY

The Morris Cerullo School of Ministry has been called "The school with a difference." During intensive training sessions, thousands receive extensive training in spiritual warfare and in how to "work the works of God."

The teaching and training during these schools goes beyond the textbooks. It takes the people beyond the realm of "head knowledge" and into "revelation knowledge." Through these sessions, there is an impartation and anointing of the Holy Spirit which mobilizes and equips the students to reach their countries with the Gospel in a demonstration of God's power.

Since 1962, when God gave Dr. Cerullo the mandate, "Son, build Me an army," more than 1.3 million national pastors, ministers, and lay people, in one hundred and thirty nations, have been trained!

DECADE OF HARVEST...

Dr. Cerullo has now launched a worldwide outreach that encompasses the globe and includes the 10-year Master Plan of Evangelism, beginning in 2001 and extending through 2010.

The major focus is "God's heartbeat-souls!" The goal is to go into the most unreached areas in every major world region, and those regions considered closed to the Gospel, and conduct crusades. This will involve mobilizing a massive army of Nationals, who have been trained, equipped, and are now ready to reap a great harvest of souls.

GLOBAL SATELLITE NETWORK SCHOOLS OF MINISTRY

Advanced, on-going training for national Christian leaders at strategic sites worldwide.

GLOBAL PRAYER STRIKE FORCE

In 1997, God spoke to Dr. Cerullo and said, "Raise up a prayer covering over the world". Since that time, an army of approximately 100,000 intercessors has been mobilized to cover the world with on-going, strategic warfare prayer and intercession. More than 500 Global Prayer Strike Force leaders in 67 different countries have been established. Thousands of Prayer Command Centers have been established in homes and churches around the world.

VICTORY WITH MORRIS CERULLO

A television outreach featured on major broadcasting stations, satellite networks, and countless cable companies in the United States, Great Britain, the Philippines, Israel, Puerto Rico, and literally around the world.

PRIME-TIME SPECIALS

Morris Cerullo World Evangelism has produced several major, prime-time television specials including *Masada, Monument to Freedom Advent I, Advent II, Philippines, A Nation In Crisis, The Rabbi, and, A Christmas Journey of Miracles.*

BOOK AND AUDIO/VIDEO CASSETTE MINISTRY

Dr. Cerullo has authored more than 200 books, and produced numerous video and audio training materials. For your free copy of our *Blessed* magazine, write to us at our ministry offices.

MORRIS CERULLO WORLD EVANGELISM

U.S.:
P. O. Box 85277
San Diego, CA 92186
(858) 277-2200
Web Site: www.mcwe.com

U.K.:
P. O. Box 277
Hemel Hempstead
Herts HP2 7DH
(01442) 232-432

CANADA:
P. O. Box 3600
Concord, Ontario
L4K 1B6
(905) 669-1758

Morris Cerullo Helpline
www.helplinetv.com

MIRACLE QUESTIONNAIRE...

After you have filled out this special questionnaire, write out the miracle you need now on the reverse side and mail it to me today.

Faith is a fact, but faith is an act!

Taking a step of faith, acting on the truths you have received, is very important NOW!

QUESTION 1: What is the circumstance in your life that cannot be met by human means?

_____
_____
_____

QUESTION 2: What are some of the thoughts you have had regarding your circumstance?

_____
_____
_____

QUESTION 3: Is God greater than this circumstance in your life?

_____
_____
_____

QUESTION 4: What is God's promise to you regarding your circumstance?

_____
_____
_____

QUESTION 5: Have you taken your eyes off your circumstance? Are you able to see your problem as a miracle opportunity?

_____
_____
_____

Over ➡

The Miracle Book

MY MIRACLE STEP...

Fill this out and
mail it to me TODAY!

...if two of you shall agree on earth as touching any thing that they shall ask, it shall be done for them of my Father which is in heaven.

(Matthew 18:19)

I need the following miracles in my life:

_____

_____

_____

_____

_____

_____

_____

signed

❏ MR. & MRS.　　❏ MR.　　❏ MRS.　　❏ MS.

NAME_____

ADDRESS _____

CITY _____ STATE OR PROVINCE _____

ZIP/POSTAL CODE _____ COUNTRY _____

PHONE _____ EMAIL _____

MY CONFESSION OF FAITH

...If thou shalt confess with thy mouth the Lord Jesus, and shalt believe in thine heart that God hath raised him from the dead, thou shalt be saved. For with the heart man believeth unto righteousness; and with the mouth confession is made unto salvation. (Romans 10: 9-10)

Congratulations! You Have Just Received The Greatest Miracle Of All!

Now that you have accepted Christ into your life, please fill out this form and return it to me. My staff and I want to pray for you. I want to send you spiritual material that will help you as you begin your new life as a born-again Christian.

❑ I have prayed the prayer for the greatest miracle in the world. I have accepted Christ as my Lord and Savior.

I HAVE A BOOK I WANT TO SEND TO YOU AS A FREE GIFT. IT WILL OPEN THE EYES OF YOUR UNDERSTANDING TO THE STRUGGLES OF LIFE AND HOW YOU CAN LIVE A VICTORIOUS NEW LIFE ONCE YOU KNOW WHAT GOD HAS PROVIDED.

❑ MR. & MRS.   ❑ MR.   ❑ MRS.   ❑ MS.
NAME_____

ADDRESS _____

CITY _____ STATE OR PROVINCE _____

ZIP/POSTAL CODE _____ COUNTRY _____

PHONE _____ EMAIL _____

Morris Cerullo World Evangelism

U.S.	CANADA	U.K.
P.O. Box 85277	P.O. Box 3600	P.O. Box 277
San Diego	Concord	Hemel Hempstead
CA 92186-5277	Ontario L4K 1B6	Herts HP2 7DH

...and God gave me a vision!

There is a greater anointing upon me now than ever before to pray for your needs.

Never before, in my more than 57 years of frontline ministry, have I carried a deeper burden for the Body of Christ than I do now. I have prayed, fasted, interceded, agonized, and fought spiritual warfare against satanic powers...

...and God gave me a vision!

A vision of Jesus Christ, our Great High Priest, praying for all your needs.

God said, *Place the needs of My people upon the altar before My presence. Jesus is praying for all their needs to be met.*

Every need, every disease, every family problem, every circumstance... God wants me to lift your need for Jesus to pray for you. Do not delay. Write all your needs on the following page and mail it to me today!

For prayer call:
1-858-435-7546

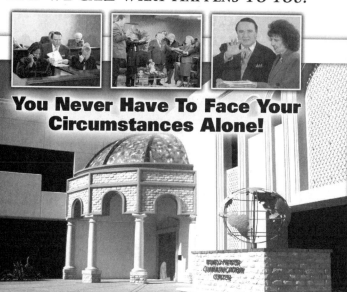